MODERN THAILAND

A Volume in the Comparative
Societies Series

OTHER TITLES IN THE COMPARATIVE SOCIETIES SERIES

MODERN THAILAND

A Volume in the Comparative Societies Series

ROBERT SLAGTER
Birmingham Southern College
Birmingham, Alabama

HAROLD R. KERBO
California Polytechnic State University
San Luis Obispo, California

Boston   Burr Ridge, IL   Dubuque, IA   Madison, WI
New York   San Francisco   St. Louis
Bangkok   Bogotá   Caracas   Lisbon   London   Madrid   Mexico City
Milan   New Delhi   Seoul   Singapore   Sydney   Taipei   Toronto

McGraw-Hill Higher Education

A Division of The McGraw-Hill Companies

MODERN THAILAND

This book is printed on acid-free paper.

1 2 3 4 5 6 7 8 9 0 DOC/DOC 9 0 9 8 7 6 5 4 3 2 1 0 9

ISBN 0-07-034428-0

Editorial director: *Phillip A. Butcher*
Sponsoring editor: *Sally Constable*
Editorial coordinator: *Kate Purcell*
Marketing manager: *Leslie A. Kraham*
Project manager: *Kimberly D. Hooker*
Production supervisor: *Rose Hepburn*
Freelance design coordinator: *Laurie J. Entringer*
Cover photo credit: *Allan Bird*
Compositor: *Shepherd, Incorporated*
Typeface: *10/12 Palatino*
Printer: *R. R. Donnelley & Sons Company*

Library of Congress Cataloging-in-Publication Data

Slagter, Robert.
    Modern Thailand / Robert Slagter, Harold R. Kerbo.
        p.   cm. — (Comparative societies series)
    Includes bibliographical references and index.
    ISBN 0-07-034428-0
    1. Thailand.   I. Kerbo, Harold R.   II. Title.   III. Series.
DS563.5.S58   2000
959.304'4—dc21   99-37248

http://www.mhhe.com

EDITOR'S PREFACE

In one of the early scenes of the movie *Reds,* the U.S. revolutionary journalist John Reed, just back from covering the beginning of World War I, is asked by a roomful of business leaders, "What is this War really about?" John Reed stands and stops all conversation with a one-word reply—"profits." Today, war between major industrial nations would disrupt profits much more than create money for a military industrial complex. Highly integrated global markets and infrastructures support the daily life of suburban families in Chicago and urban squatter settlements in Bombay. These ties produce a social and economic ecology that transcends political and cultural boundaries.

The world is a very different place than it was for our parents and grandparents. Those rare epic events of world war certainly invaded their everyday lives and futures, but we now find that daily events thousands of miles away, in countries large and small, have a greater impact on North Americans than ever before, with the speed of this impact multiplied many times in recent decades. Our standard of living, jobs, and even prospects of living in a healthy environment have never before been so dependent on outside forces.

Yet there is much evidence that North Americans have less easy access to good information about the outside world than even a few years ago. Since the end of the Cold War, newspaper and television coverage of events in other countries has dropped dramatically. It is difficult to put much blame on the mass media, however: International news seldom sells any more. There is simply less interest.

It is not surprising, then, that Americans know comparatively little about the outside world. A recent *Los Angeles Times* survey provides a good example: People in eight countries were asked five basic questions about current events of the day. Americans were dead last in their knowledge, trailing people from Canada, Mexico, England, France, Spain, Germany, and Italy.* It is also not surprising that the annual report published by the Swiss World Economic Forum always ranks American executives quite low in their international experience and understanding.

Such ignorance harms American competitiveness in the world economy in many ways. But there is much more. Seymour Martin Lipset put it nicely in one of his recent books: "Those who know only one country know no country" (Lipset 1996: 17). Considerable time spent in a foreign

---

*For example, while only 3 percent of Germans missed all five questions, 37 percent of the Americans did (*Los Angeles Times,* March 16, 1994).

country is one of the best stimulants for a sociological imagination: Studying or doing research in other countries makes us realize how much we
really, in fact, have learned about our own society in the process. Seeing
other social arrangements, ways of doing things, and foreign perspectives
allows for far greater insight into the familiar, our own society. This is
also to say that ignorance limits solutions to many of our own serious social problems. How many Americans, for example, are aware that levels
of poverty are much lower in all other advanced nations and that the
workable government services in those countries keep poverty low? Likewise, how many Americans are aware of alternative means of providing
health care and quality education or reducing crime?

We can take heart in the fact that sociology in the United States has
become more comparative in recent decades. A comparative approach, of
course, was at the heart of classical European sociology during the 1800s.
But as sociology was transported from Europe to the United States early
in the 20th century, it lost much of this comparative focus. In recent years,
sociology journals have published more comparative research. There are
large data sets with samples from many countries around the world in research seeking general laws on issues such as the causes of social mobility
or political violence, all very much in the tradition of Durkheim. But we
also need much more of the old Max Weber. His was a qualitative historical and comparative perspective (Smelser 1976; Ragin and Zaret 1983).
Weber's methodology provides a richer understanding of other societies,
a greater recognition of the complexity of social, cultural, and historical
forces shaping each society. Ahead of his time in many ways, C. Wright
Mills was planning a qualitative comparative sociology of world regions
just before his death in 1961 (Horowitz 1983: 324). [Too few American sociologists have yet to follow in his footsteps.]

Following these trends, sociology textbooks in the United States
have also become more comparative in content in recent years. And
while this tendency must be applauded, it is not enough. Typically, there
is an example from Japan here, another from Germany there, and so on,
haphazardly for a few countries in different subject areas as the writer's
knowledge of these bits and pieces allows. What we need are the text-
book equivalents of a richer Weberian comparative analysis, a qualitative
comparative analysis of the social, cultural, and historical forces that
have combined to make relatively unique societies around the world. It
is this type of comparative material that can best help people in the
United States overcome their lack of understanding about other countries and allow them to see their own society with much greater insight.

The Comparative Societies Series, of which this book is a part, has
been designed as a small step in filling this need. We have currently selected 12 countries on which to focus: Japan, Thailand, Switzerland, Mexico, South Africa, Hungary, Germany, China, India, Iran, Brazil, and Rus-
sia. We selected these countries as representatives of major world regions

and cultures, and each will be examined in separate books written by talented sociologists. All of these basic sociological issues and topics will be covered: Each book will begin with a look at the important historical and geographical forces shaping the society, then turn to basic aspects of social organization and culture. From there each book will proceed to examine the political and economic institutions of the specific country, along with the social stratification, the family, religion, education, and finally urbanization, demography, social problems, and social change.

Although each volume in the Comparative Societies Series is of necessity brief to allow for use as supplementary readings in standard sociology courses, we have tried to assure that this brief coverage provides students with sufficient information to better understand each society, as well as their own. The ideal would be to transport every student to another country for a period of observation and learning. Realizing the unfortunate impracticality of this ideal, we hope to do the next best thing—to at least mentally move these students to a country very different from their own, provide something of the everyday reality of the people in these other countries, and demonstrate how the tools of sociological analysis can help them see these societies as well as their own with much greater understanding.

Harold R. Kerbo
San Luis Obispo, CA
June 1997

AUTHORS' PREFACE

To the extent people from Western countries know anything about Thailand, they most likely have positive images, promoted by the tourism industry and the recent Hollywood movie *The Beach*, of beautiful tropical beaches (as at the islands of Phuket, Samui, or Pi Pi where the movie was made), or the negative images dominating the Western mass media, such as low-paid workers, prostitution, and AIDS. The reality of Thailand is much more complex than these simplistic images. It is a country of great beauty, and the Western fascination with the exotic or negative is often unfair and frequently misleading.

Yes, Thailand is a developing country with a large unskilled labor force, working for an average of $5 per day at the end of the 1990s. However, unlike many, or even most, developing countries Thailand's economy has been developing steadily since the early 1960s (and continues despite the "Asian economic crisis" beginning in 1997), and the Thai workers making $5 a day at the end of the 1990s were making much less only 10 years ago. Again, contrary to common assumptions, the outside exploitation of cheap labor by corporations from rich nations is not making the poor poorer; since the 1950s the proportion of Thai people living in poverty has dropped from around 50 percent of the population to only about 13 percent at the end of the 1990s.

There is indeed a large sex industry in Thailand, with brothels to be found all over the country; and Thai people as well as tourists flock to these places, especially in Bangkok. Thai people will sadly admit that today there are more prostitutes than Buddhist monks in Thailand. In contrast to this image of rampant prostitution and sexual immorality, it must be recognized that young Thai women are much more modest in their behavior, with respect to sexual activity and dress, than women in Western countries. And as we will see, when it comes to opportunities in the workplace and professions, Thai women are in some respects ahead of their sisters in many Western nations, including the United States. Although extensive prostitution is usually assumed to be associated with low status and power for women, this is not necessarily so in Thailand.

One common and interesting indicator of gender-role differences in Thailand is that until this century Thais did not have family names. While many traditional agricultural societies were patrilineal with the male line dominant and the male family name passed from generation to generation, this was not the case in Thailand. It was only through increasing contact with more powerful and threatening Western nations, however, that the king in the early 20th century decided that Thais needed last names. Although they were required to have them, then and today Thais have not warmed to the system of family names. They continue to use primarily first names only, as well as what we might call cute nicknames such as "little bird."[1]

As we will see throughout the coming pages, Thailand often appears full of contradictions. The country and its people challenge many of our assumptions about human nature, conditions in developing countries, and even the old stereotypes about Asian people and their cultures. Because of this, an examination of Thai society and culture can make us confront our assumptions on these and other topics and perhaps lead us to begin to look at the world in new and different ways. We think it is useful to study Thailand because it is a very interesting place, because a focus on Thailand is beneficial for learning more about the nature of societies in general, and because we can learn more about our own by comparing it to Thailand.

This little book about modern Thailand begins with an introduction to the place and its people before turning to more detail about Thai culture and social organization. Chapters that follow will introduce you to some important aspects of Thai history, the basic social institutions in Thai society—the political system, economy, family, religion, and education. Concluding chapters will focus on social problems confronting Thailand today and the process of social change. Throughout these chapters there will be explicit comparisons to the United States and other Western nations, and at times to other Asian nations. In every chapter our goal is not only to help you understand the fascinating and sometimes puzzling people who live in Thailand today but also to understand something about the basic nature of societies and humans in general and in the process learn much more about yourself and the society of which you are a part.

Finally, we would like to extend our sincere thanks to several people in the United States, Thailand, and other countries who have helped us better understand Thailand in general and specifically helped us in writing this book. Our old friend Uthai Dulyakasem at Silpakorn University, helpful in many ways over the years, aided us in obtaining some of the information used in various places in this book. Much the same can be said for Nikom Tangkapipop, Pornlerd Uampuang, and Kanit Kheovichal, also at Silpakorn University in Bangkok, and Nakorn Pathom. At the Prince of Songkla University in Hat Yai, Sommart Chulapongse and Jongpid Sirirat were gracious hosts while we were living and teaching at their university; they also helped us understand many aspects of Thai society. Seksin Srivatananukulkit of Chiang Mai University also provided valuable insights.

We would also like to thank Volker Bornschier at the University of Zurich and past president of the World Society Foundation for a generous research grant that allowed us to conduct research in Thailand for two years from 1995 to 1996. Along these lines we are also obligated to various people associated with the Institute for International Education and Fulbright offices in Thailand for their support during our Fulbright study at Chulalongkorn University, Bangkok, during 1990.

At McGraw-Hill we would first like to thank Amy Smeltzley, who got behind the Comparative Societies Series in its early stages of planning; and then our current editor, Sally Constable, and her assistant, Kate Purcell, who have kept us on track and put up with our long delays; and finally Kimberly Hooker, who as always did a superb job in the editing and production process with McGraw-Hill. In various ways all of the above individuals helped make this book a reality.

Robert Slagter
Harold R. Kerbo

TABLE OF CONTENTS

Chapter 4

The Thai Political System   49

Chapter 5

Social Stratification in Thailand   61

Chapter 6

Religion in Thailand   78

Chapter 7

The Family and Education in Thailand   90

Chapter 8

Social Change and Social Problems in Modern Thailand   105

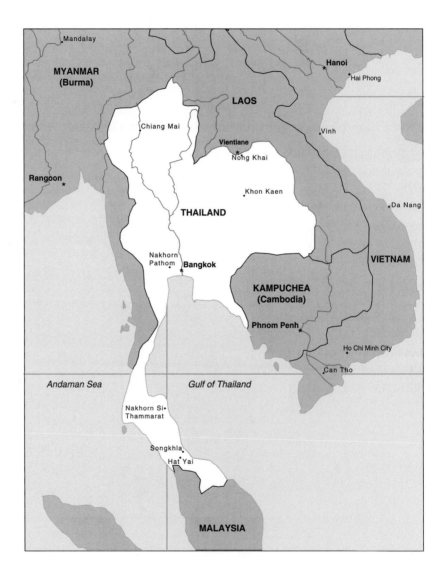

Mandalay

MYANMAR
(Burma)

Chiang Mai

LAOS

Hanoi

Hai Phong

Vinh

Vientiane
Nong Khai

Rangoon

Khon Kaen

THAILAND

Da Nang

Nakhorn
Pathom

Bangkok

VIETNAM

KAMPUCHEA
(Cambodia)

Phnom Penh

Ho Chi Minh City

Can Tho

Andaman Sea

Gulf of Thailand

Nakhorn Si
Thammarat

Songkhla
Hat Yai

MALAYSIA

CHAPTER 1

Modern Thailand: An Introduction

THE PLACE

Thailand is a part of the region we refer to today as Southeast Asia. In typical fashion, most earlier descriptions of Asia contained Western biases: The "far East" was not the far East unless you were in Europe; "further India" assumes you are on the other side of India and that Southeast Asia has much in common with India; and "Asia of the monsoons" is a clear misnomer for much of the area (Osborne 1995: 4). The name Southeast Asia, however, does well in locating Thailand among the Asian nations that are south of China and Japan and east of the huge Indian subcontinent. As can be seen in the map of Thailand, on the west and north Thailand borders Burma (or Myanmar as the current military dictators of Burma insist the country be called), with Laos on the north and east, and Cambodia further down the east. Thailand extends southward along the Malay peninsula to its border with Malaysia. The other large countries that make up the Southeast Asian region include Vietnam, Indonesia, and the Philippines.

There are some common characteristics shared by all countries in this Southeast Asian region, but there are also many significant differences. In contrast to another general image shared by most non-Asians, not all Asian countries are alike; in fact, it may be that there are greater differences among the nations of East and Southeast Asia than among European nations.

One characteristic generally shared by all nations of Southeast Asia, however, is climate. The entire region is tropical or subtropical, with some remaining dense jungle and rain forest, extensive rainfall, and consistently high temperatures. Upon first entering Thailand, in fact, it is often the heat and high humidity that form the first impressions of Western visitors. Such visitors may wonder why early people would want to settle in such a hot and humid country in the first place. But after traveling around

1

the country even briefly a very basic answer will come to mind: food. Like other countries in the region, Thailand is a virtual greenhouse; in the hot and humid climate many varieties of plants thrive, and even today outside of the major cities there is an abundance of food growing naturally. It takes a major human-created tragedy, such as the Khmer Rouge revolutionary experiment in Cambodia, to provoke starvation in Southeast Asia. In the case of Thailand, climate and social organization have combined to make the country a rich center of agriculture production and exporter of food.

Not all of Thailand, however, is made up of hills covered with dense jungle rendering the country a popular place to film Vietnam War movies. In the center and northeast of Thailand there are broad flat plains, which are ideal for rice cultivation. This is especially true of the central region, which has much more rainfall than the northeast. Bangkok, the national capital of Thailand, is set near the southern end of a flat delta formed by the mighty Chao Phraya River. It is rice agriculture, particularly wet rice, that made civilization possible in Thailand, and this type of agriculture has shaped some of the basic characteristics of the Thai society and culture examined in later chapters.

THE PEOPLE

Just over 60 million people live in Thailand today in an area about the size of Texas. Thus, again contrary to popular assumptions in the West about most Asian countries, Thailand is not a particularly crowded nation. Crowding is a problem in the capital and central city of Bangkok, but that is a matter of choice rather than a problem of overpopulation. Officially, Bangkok has 6 million people, or 10 percent of the population of the whole country, but in actuality there are closer to 10 million people living in the city. The problems of managing that city and its rapid growth, which is an urban planner's nightmare, are considered later in Chapter 8.

With respect to the total population of Thailand, over 70 percent are ethnic Tais, the dominant cultural and **ethnic group** today. The Tai moved into what is now Thailand from China about 1,000 years ago. People have lived in the region for at least 40,000 years, however, and there is now some evidence that the Bronze Age actually began in Thailand almost 6,000 years ago (Shearer 1989: 198; Wyatt 1984: 3–4). While the Tai is the largest group, Thailand's population is made up of a rich mixture of ethnic Asian groups, including many **hill tribe** people with quite different traditions, ethnic Chinese, Laos, and Malays (who are mostly Muslim, in contrast to the Buddhist traditions of the other ethnic groups) and other nationalities from Southeast Asia. One of the most important characteristics of Thailand that other people around the world would do well to understand and emulate is the relative racial and ethnic harmony in the kingdom despite this rich diversity of peoples (Fallows 1994: 291).

An additional important factor in Thailand's history is its experience with the Western nations. In terms of level of development there are over 130 nation-states in the world classified as less developed nations (LDCs), including Thailand. Of these countries, only four—Afghanistan, Liberia, Turkey, and Thailand—were not subject to colonization by one of the more developed nations (Hadenius 1992). While all of the other nations of East and Southeast Asia experienced some form of colonization—Vietnam, Cambodia, and Laos by France; Burma and Malaysia by England; and Indonesia by the Dutch—Thailand escaped despite its strategic location and the fact that it was militarily and economically weaker than many of its neighbors. As a result, throughout the 20th century Thailand has remained an island of relative tranquility as nationalist anticolonial revolutions were waged in nations all around her. Today there is less resentment and anger toward foreigners among Thais since they did not experience the humiliation of colonialism.

Equally important, Thailand's ability to remain free of direct colonial domination meant that its indigenous development was relatively less influenced by foreigners and its traditions and culture are better preserved than those in neighboring countries that have been disrupted by colonialism. In fact, many of the positive characteristics found in Thailand today can be related in one way or another to the Thais' ability to remain free of the Western powers (Muscat 1994: 28; Kulick and Wilson 1996: 5; Girling 1981: 163).

THAI CULTURE AND SOCIAL ORGANIZATION

We now consider some aspects of this Thai culture and its traditions, in particular some of the core values and beliefs of the Thai people. We describe Thai culture first by focusing on those elements that Thais share with many other Asian peoples and then examining other values and beliefs that distinguish the Thais and create the complex and sometimes puzzling mix of behaviors and practices one finds in Thailand.

We should begin with a few examples. As a foreigner traveling in Thailand you are likely to immediately notice many customs not found in Western nations. For example, in a variety of settings you might notice people greeting each other with a **wai**—hands together, fingers pointing up, held about chest-high, and accompanied by a bow. Looking carefully you might also notice that all wais are not equal; sometimes the hands are raised a little higher, the bow is a little deeper. These subtle differences are evidence of one of the most important aspects of Thai culture, **hierarchy.** To a much greater extent than in the United States and other Western nations, in Thailand there is a well-defined social hierarchy that is recognized and acknowledged by people in a wide variety of social settings. These differences in wais (greetings) are just one of the ways relative positions in the hierarchy are acknowledged. The person giving a wai just a bit more emphatically, as you might expect, is the subordinate person, while the one whose wai is more perfunctory with hands held lower than the head is of higher rank.

After befriending Thais you have the opportunity to observe another element of Thai culture, the extremely *strong sense of self,* or a preference for **individualism,** which can lead Thai people to be rather spontaneous and free. One of your friends might suddenly quit a job (or just not show up for work) to go traveling with a friend, visit up country, or do something else for a good time. Here we come to one of the puzzling contrasts in Thai culture: Societies with well-defined hierarchies normally do not feature such individualistic behavior. Japan, for example, is more consistent in this respect, with both a well-defined status ranking and less of what can be defined as individualistic behavior. Thai society, therefore, has been described as "first and foremost hierarchically structured where individualism and social relations are of the utmost importance" (Suntaree 1990:131–138). This contradiction between hierarchy and individualism is indicated in two Thai proverbs: "dogs will not bite you if you follow the social superior" and "to be able to do what one wants is to be a real Thai" (Akin 1996: xx).

A third key element of Thai culture is important to recognize: avoidance of conflict, or maintaining smooth social relations. This is the lubricant of Thai society. A logical question may have occurred to you: With many individualistic people placed in a complex set of hierarchical relationships, how can constant conflict be avoided? For the most part, social order in social interactions is maintained by **norms,** or rules, stressing politeness, a calm and even temperament, modesty, and the avoidance of direct confrontation. In other words, at least on the surface, people should act as if all is well and people are getting along, even if such is not really the case.

Let's consider another example: If you were the manager of a foreign corporation in Thailand, you might call a meeting of the Thai staff hoping to discuss some problems the organization was experiencing. Instead of the open and frank discussion you anticipated, however, it is likely that you would find everyone quite reluctant to speak up; and if someone did, his or her ideas would be expressed only in a vague and general way (Holmes and Suchada 1995). Disappointed in the meeting, you would probably be surprised that over the next few days many of the same people spoke to you privately, giving an excellent analysis of the problem topic of the earlier meeting and proposing excellent workable solutions. In this case you would be experiencing all three aspects of Thai culture noted above: the emphasis on smooth social relations, showing respect to authority figures, and the avoidance of confrontation and injury to anyone's honor, or a loss of **face.**

UNDERSTANDING CULTURE AND DIFFERENCES

These examples are manifestations of **culture** in the behaviors of daily life. The component of culture more difficult to ascertain is what can't be seen, the patterns of thinking that are the motivations for the actions. All societies have a culture of everyday life composed of two elements. One is mental, the internalized subjective values that guide behavior. The other is external, the regularized practices that are a reflection of those values. One definition of culture refers to it as the collective programming of the mind and the everyday practices associated with it that distinguish the members of one group or category of people from another (Hofstede 1991: 5). To help us better understand modern Thailand, we will examine Thai culture using the above definition. We take a building-block approach: First we describe the "programming of the mind," beginning with the most basic assumptions shaping Thai culture. Then we present more specific components of the programming, the values that guide everyday behavior. Finally, we present some of the behavioral patterns characteristic of Thai culture, which are the manifestation of the mental programs that guide Thais through everyday life.

A Caution on the Concept of Culture

Having said all of this, though, we must present a few words of caution. First, cultural values are rather vague: In practice they need interpretation to show how they apply. Second, cultural values are sometimes subject to change; they are not so deeply ingrained within individuals and societies as is often assumed. As we will see, Thailand, like many other Asian countries, has been in a process of rapid change in recent decades, and in many ways the young people are different from their parents. Third, we are describing the culture of a society. Within that society any particular individual may adhere more or less to the model of culture that pertains to the entire society.

It is also easy to exaggerate what are described as the "cultural features" of any society. All cultural systems are complex and inconsistent; the very opposite tendency can often be seen existing alongside the cultural feature being explained.

With these cautions in mind, however, we can look at some of the most general aspects of Thai cultural values that do influence the society, the behavior of Thai people, and much of what happens in Thailand today.

WORLDVIEWS

Worldviews develop as people "answer" fundamental questions about the nature of humans and human societies. At the most abstract level, these assumptions are behind many of the more specific values and beliefs found in human cultures, as well as sociological theories about societies (Kuhn 1971; Ritzer 1996; Kerbo 1996). The first question involves human nature: Are people basically good or bad, cooperative and sharing, or selfish and acquisitive? Depending on the answers, every society develops ways to manage conflict between, and facilitate cooperation among, its members. Another important question has to do with people's relationship to nature: Is nature benevolent and therefore to be adapted to? Or is nature threatening and capricious, which means it has to be dominated? The answers to the questions regarding nature shape how a society determines the best way to obtain basic needs such as food, shelter, and security, as well as to satisfy desires for leisure, fun, and self-expression. Finally, every society has to develop an idea about time: What is the relationship between the past, present, and future? Which is more important and therefore the greater focus of interest in a society? The answers to these questions comprise a world view, a way of thinking about the world that influences how individuals and the society as a whole operate (Kluckholm and Strodtbeck 1960).

In the Thai worldview, people are seen as neither essentially good nor bad but capable of either. As we will see in a later chapter, the Buddhist idea of **kamma** is integrated into the Thai worldview and injects two somewhat contradictory ideas. Following the Buddhist belief in reincarnation, on the one hand, a person's fate is determined by the kamma derived from past lives. But on the other hand, humans can control much of their own destiny because what an individual does in this life determines that person's kamma. The Thai view, contrary to Western ideas of humans as inherently bad and in need of control by laws and salvation by a deity, is that humans are essentially good and need only the opportunity and direction to realize that goodness. For Thai people, doing good is a matter of wisdom, doing evil a matter of stupidity, and every person is capable of doing either (Suntaree 1991, Mulder 1994).

With respect to the natural world or environment, in Western cultures a distinction is generally made between human nature and the natural world, with humans viewed as in opposition to nature, thus attempting to subdue and control it. The contrasting Thai worldview considers that humans, nature, and a supernatural world are all blended together in a unified whole. Humans have their place in the natural scheme of things just like animals and spirits, and both are humanity's brethren. Because people are considered a part of nature, they are subject to it. There is much about nature that cannot be controlled, but having a place in nature, humans can adapt and extract from nature what is needed for survival (Suntaree 1991). As points of contrast, the Japanese worldview tends further toward perceiving man as subject to nature, with the individual's fortune in life being due to forces beyond his or her control. In the United States, individuals are viewed as more able to control their own destiny and nature is to be subdued and conquered. The Thai view falls between these two cultures, with people seen as less subjected to nature than in the Japanese view but more so than in the United States.

Spirit House—A typical spirit house in central Thailand. In front of the house are the flowers, water, and incense that demonstrate the giver's respect for the resident spirit (see p. 85).

In Western industrialized societies like the United States, time is thought of as sequential or linear. With this orientation, time is viewed as a series of passing events, each essentially discrete, and there is an awareness of the passing minutes, hours, and days. The present is most important, with less awareness of the past and considerable emphasis on the future. In many less developed countries, including Thailand, the orientation to time is synchronic and the past, present, and future are seen as highly interrelated, with each considered equally important. In societies with a sequential view of time, as in the United States, activities are done in sequence, first one task then another. There is great emphasis on punctuality and considerable urgency about getting things done; many interactions between people are formal and abrupt.

In a society such as Thailand with a synchronic view of time, activities are done in parallel, and there is less emphasis on punctuality, more spontaneity, and always time for interaction with other people. As an example, if you were to visit an American professor in her office while she was on the phone, she might acknowledge your presence with a gesture but she would complete the phone conversation before giving full attention to you. In Thailand, it is probable that in the same circumstance the phone conversation would be interrupted for a warm greeting and a little conversation and then the professor would converse with you and the person on the phone simultaneously, or the professor would at least continue to acknowledge your presence while still on the telephone.

SOCIAL VALUES

In addition to worldviews or paradigm assumptions are **values,** which are more specific and have two components. **Terminal values** are the goals of existence and focus on what is desirable for the society and individuals. **Instrumental values** are the socially preferable modes of conduct (behaviors, practices) for achieving the goals defined by the terminal values. Terminal values are part of the mental programming that signals what people should strive for; instrumental values specify the socially appropriate ways of attaining the desired. One of the sociological masters referred to these two types of values as the "goals" and the "means," respectively (Merton 1957).

The most systematic examination of Thai social values, with data based on national samples, has been done by the Thai social psychologist Suntaree Komin (1991). It is useful to begin by noting some of the differences Suntaree found between American and Thai values. As terminal values, Americans rated a world at peace, family security, freedom, equality, self-respect, and happiness as most important. Thais rated national security, religious/spiritual life, a comfortable life, family happiness/security, "brotherhood spirit," self-esteem, and success in life as most important. While international and family security are important in both cultures, freedom is less important in Thailand, and the equality value does not emerge at all. And though Americans highly value self-respect and happiness at the individual level, Thais value self-esteem, comfortableness in life, and brotherhood spirit. We can say that the American values are more *individually oriented* with the individual's respect earned and enjoyed, whereas the Thai values are more *externally oriented,* with esteem dictated by the society; for the Thais, "brotherhood spirit" emphasizes social relations, and comfortableness means a lack of material concerns. In another study, Rokeach (1996) characterized American society as "individualistic egalitarian." Thai society is *individualistic and hierarchical,* which, as noted already, can lead to confusion in understanding the Thai society and culture.

There are also important differences between the instrumental values of American and Thai cultures. American instrumental values are focused almost exclusively on the individual in terms of self-assertiveness and self-achievement. The emphasis is on being honest, responsible, ambitious, broad-minded, and courageous. Americans are expected to make their own place in society through individual effort. The Thai value system also places emphasis on the individual and independence, but only within the context of appropriate social relations in which the feelings and needs of others are always taken into account.

In addition to the above, Suntaree's (1991) research has found what Thai's call **bunkhun,** or grateful relationships, to be very important, especially given the tension between individual ego and hierarchy described above. Bunkhun relationships are personal, involve the exchange of favors or benefits, and are mutually beneficial. For a subordinate person, doing a favor for a superior creates a sense of obligation on the part of the superior; the favor must be recognized and reciprocated. In this manner the subordinate person derives both respect and advantage from the subordinate position. The doing of the favor also indicates respect for the superior and, in creating the obligation to repay the favor, provides the opportunity for the superior to demonstrate the desirable qualities, the goodness and "brotherhood spirit," that are thought to be inherent in a person of superior status. When the favor is repaid, however, things are not equal, for now the subordinate owes a favor. In this way, over time, stable and mutually beneficial relationships between subordinates and superiors are established and maintained with little chance of conflict.

Such relationships are the basis of the one thing almost all observers of Thai society agree upon—the prevalence of patron-client relationships. The whole of Thai society can be thought of as a vast network of relationships between superiors and subordinates based in large measure on bunkhun. While in their ideal and common form these relationships are mutually beneficial, they can be exploitive (Akin 1993).

Finally, we conclude with another important Thai value that Westerners always find interesting. As noted in beginning, the avoidance of conflict is one of the key instrumental values in the Thai society. To maintain smooth social relations and thus avoid conflict, much interpersonal communication is very indirect. For example, the Tourist Authority of Thailand has promoted the country as the "land of smiles," and certainly smiling is a more common form of communication than in the West. Often foreigners interpret smiling as indicating happiness and satisfaction, and they conclude that Thais are an inherently happy people with few cares or worries. Such an interpretation, however, is completely false. Smiles are an intentional means of communication, and there are names in Thai for the types of smiles. The word for smile is **yim** and examples of the various types are *yim sao,* the sad smile, and *yim haeng,* the dry smile that indicates realization of something owed or that needs to be done but will not be. Of course smiles can indicate real happiness, *yim thang nam taa,* and or perhaps pure politeness, *yim thak thaai* (Holmes and Suchada 1995). Once again, smiling is a form of nonverbal communication that reduces overt conflict, maintains honor, and facilitates the smooth social relations that are so desired and important in Thai life.

ASIAN VALUE SYSTEMS

Before leaving this discussion of culture and values, it is useful to consider some of the broad differences between Asian and Western cultures more generally and an explanation for the differences. At the most general level of value preferences, the West is commonly described as having an **individualistic value system,** while Asia is described as having a **collectivist value system.** Most simply, this means that the group is generally more important in Asia, while the individual is more important in the West. Not all Western countries are alike with the degree to which values such as individualism are stressed, nor are all Asian countries alike with respect in the degree to which collectivism is stressed (Hofstede 1991: 53). But as such generalities go, this one tends to be quite valid.

In his famous study of about 15,000 people from 53 countries, for example, Hofstede (1991) found the United States highest on his individualism index with a score of 91(100 is a perfect score), while Thailand scored 20, tied with two other nations at the ranks of 39–41, among the lowest scores of all nations in the sample of 53. Australia, England, Canada, the Netherlands, and New Zealand are ranked just below the United States on this index, while countries such as Singapore, Hong Kong, South Korea, Taiwan, and Malaysia score close to Thailand.

As industrialization was rapidly changing European societies in the 18th and 19th centuries, many of the best social scientists of the time—such as Emile Durkheim, Max Weber, and Ferdinand Tonnies—were asking questions about the changing value orientations and social organization of these societies, speculating about how societies would survive with the breakdown of traditional authority structures and growing individualism. A totally individualistic society, a society with everyone going their own way, considering only their own selfish interests, these social scientists knew, would not work: There would be only destructive conflict and anarchy. However flawed some of his ideas, Sigmund Freud, the great interpreter of the Western mind, also outlined this dilemma of human societies in one of his greatest books, *Civilization and Its Discontents,* in 1930. Some means of organization and compromise must be attained between the conflicting interests of the group and the individual.

The Western industrialized societies, especially the United States, evolved toward allowing ever more freedom to the individual (Lipset 1996). The individual, of course, must continue to have responsibilities toward, and even make some sacrifices for, important groups—the family and work groups, for example. But as much as possible, in these Western nations, and to the greatest extent in the United States,[2] value preferences suggest that individuals should be given as much freedom and independence as possible. Asian collectivist cultures, in contrast, require more sacrifice for group needs and place more restraints on what the individual may do in satisfying individual desires. All of this affects not only the individual's relation to small groups but also the individual's relation to the broader community and nation. As we will see in coming chapters, the more collectivist value orientation in Thailand affects much of what they do.

The standard explanation for differences between the more individualistic West and the more collectivist East is worth considering briefly. At base, the explanation may seem simplistic, perhaps even absurd, because it has to do with what people eat, what people in the West versus those in the East have most depended upon for survival over the centuries.[3] It is not, however, the nutrients or even chemicals in this food, but rather, how the food must be produced. In contrast to the cultivation of cereal crops such as wheat in Western civilizations, a long history of wet rice cultivation has helped establish a collectivist value orientation across Asia. Wet rice cultivation is labor intensive, requiring group cooperation in community projects to get the water in and out of the field at the right time during the growing seasons. Thus, out of necessity, values favoring group unity and control over the individual developed through the many centuries of dependence upon wet rice cultivation for food.

Thai "Individualism"

We have already noted, however, that Thailand presents us with a more complex case of what seems to be a mixture of collectivism and individualism (Cohen 1991: 36–46; Girling 1981: 41). After spending considerable time in another Asian country, such as Japan, and then moving to Thailand, you clearly notice some differences—differences that are not easy to explain at first. Yes, the Thais, when compared to Westerners, are more group oriented. But, then again, you accumulate observations that make you unsure of such a collectivist characterization of Thai people. They do seem more independent, they like that the name Thailand means "land of the free," and they seem more spontaneous in their behavior. You might see an auto accident and observe that Thai people arriving on the scene seem to act quickly and independently to the situation, rather uncharacteristic for some Asian people who are more likely to respond more slowly, hoping that some type of authority figure will emerge to tell them what should be done.

Some of the first Western social scientists studying Thailand established the concept of the country as being a "loose structured society," indicating this relative Thai individualism compared to other Asian societies (Embree 1950; Phillips 1966). But this concept of a loose structured society to characterize Thailand has come under much criticism recently with more research on Thailand (Suntaree 1990). In place of this characterization, more social scientists now see a better explanation of the mix of Thai collectivism and individualism by referring to personal versus impersonal relations in the Thai society (Mulder 1994: 43). In more personal relations, such as those formed in families or even long-term work groups, there is more of an Asian-style collectivism, or group orientation, in Thailand. Much like in Japan, for example, these groups strictly order the behavior of their members, and a firm authority structure exists that must be respected. With more impersonal relations in the society, however, Thais are more independent and free. The previous example of behavior on the streets of Thailand can again be instructive. Japanese people are much more likely to follow traffic laws; for Thais, traffic laws seem merely suggestions to be violated whenever it fits their interests and the police appear nowhere around.

THAI SOCIAL ORGANIZATION: A CONCLUSION

We can conclude this chapter by applying some of what we have learned above to some traditional sociological concepts related to social organization in societies. In all societies, social relationships can be viewed as falling along a continuum from the most personal of relationships within the family to the least personal in anonymous onetime interactions with others. Sociologists have long called groups made up of the first type of relations **primary groups,** while groups with more temporary and impersonal relations are called **secondary groups.** In primary groups such as the family, personal relationships are close, emotionally charged, and diffuse, which means they serve many functions simultaneously (psychological support, material support, etc.). In secondary groups, such as temporary work groups, relationships are generally limited only to the tasks at hand, with very little emotional involvement between individuals expected.

Applying these originally Western sociological concepts to Asian countries we find a Western bias—a bias not so much in the concepts themselves, but how they have been applied. In Asian societies with collectivist orientations as described above, the group is much more important, and this generally means not only the usual primary groups such as the family are important, but also work groups become more important. In essence, we can say that in Asian societies such as Japan and Thailand, what would be secondary groups in the West, such as work groups, are likely to become primary groups (Kerbo and McKinstry 1998). For instance, in a boss-employee relationship in Japan and Thailand, the boss is expected not only to exercise power and give direction but also to provide protection and become involved in many personal affairs such as marriages and funerals, giving support and advice (Lincoln and Kalleberg 1990; Holmes and Suchada 1995). Similarly, relations between the employees are more personal, and Thais may view the workplace as a type of family satisfying a variety of emotional and social needs, in addition to supplying a salary. The Japanese likely describe their relations with others as "wet" relations (involving this emotional content), whereas the Thais have many terms describing their relations with others having the root word *heart.*

Thus, we can conclude by again noting that in contrast to people in Western societies, Thai people do tend to form stronger and more emotional ties with others, and the group is more important. There is the greater individualism shown by Thai people in many more impersonal situations, but when it comes to the basic structure of the society, Thailand is still a collectivist society. There are other important characteristics of Thai society and social organization: For example, we will see that Thais tend to be very religious people. A particular type of **Buddhism** has been combined with **animism,** beliefs that emphasize the importance of taming spirit forces in the society and using them for human interests. These beliefs and their effects will be examined in some detail in our chapter on religion in Thailand. But as we move through the topics to follow in this book, from politics and economic organizations, to the family, religion, and education, we will find more often than not a group-oriented society that contrasts to Western societies, especially the United States. And with our preliminary examination of Thai culture and social organization behind us, we are now ready to make this move to other important topics about modern Thailand.

CHAPTER 2

A Brief History of Thailand

Two of the most impressive places to visit in Thailand today are the ruins of the ancient capitals of **Ayudhya** and **Sukothai.** In many dozens of archeological sites around these two cities one finds the remains of many temples and palace buildings, just small remnants of the original structures with their underlying brickwork exposed, but still beautiful with their style influenced by the old Sri Lankan and Cambodian civilizations. Around and inside the structures can be found hundreds of artifacts, including Buddha images. Most have suffered some damage from years of neglect and looting, and many of the Buddha images have their heads broken off. Unfortunately, much of this damage is the result of the demands of a market created by Western tourists and museums. The still impressive ruins, however, make it easy to imagine the original beauty and grandeur of these two old capitals, especially after seeing the breathtaking beauty of the current Grand Palace and Wat Phra Kaew in central Bangkok today.

Reflecting upon the exotic images of these old capitals, one gets the impression that they are very old indeed. The first of these old capitals, Sukothai, does date back to the 13th century, but as civilizations go, this is rather recent (Girling 1981; Pfeiffer 1977; Redman 1978). As we will see, there were some smaller kingdoms that preceded these of the Thais, but again we are not even close to the thousands of years of the Chinese civilization, or of those in Egypt or even Rome. Europe was already emerging from its Dark Ages in a revival of Western civilization before the Thai civilization that led to modern Thailand got its start. During this relatively brief time, from the 14th century to the 20th, however, the Thai civilization emerged and developed rapidly. And it was of course this civilization that laid the foundation for what is Thailand today (Keyes 1989; Wyatt 1984; Osborne 1995).

In this chapter we will take a brief look at early Thai history so that we can better understand contemporary Thai people and the society in which they live. We will quickly move to the periods of Sukothai and Ayudhya to describe the contributions of their kings and common people that shape Thai society today. But before we do so we need to understand more about what preceded, where the Thais came from, and who they were.

WHO ARE THE THAIS?

The word **Thai** derives from the **Tai,** an ethnic, cultural, and linguistic group dispersed from southern China to northeastern India and throughout Southeast Asia (Wyatt 1984; Osborne 1995). The largest population of these early Tai eventually ended up in what is Thailand today. The earliest records of the Tai place them in southern China and northern Vietnam (Terwiel 1991: 11–12). As their population increased, the Tais expanded inland into southern China during the first millennium A.D. An attempt by the Chinese to bring an end to the autonomous status of the Tai people and bring them under direct control was most likely the cause of the eventual Tai migration into Southeast Asia. As the Tais moved into the lowland valleys of this region, they conquered the indigenous peoples and imposed their language and culture on them, but they also adopted elements of the local peoples' culture, most notably Buddhism.

By the 13th century the Tai were the dominant group in the river valleys of northern and central Southeast Asia. Among the subgroups of Tai are Lao (Laos) and Shan (Burma), with links between the groups evident in language, as each group's dialect is partially comprehensible to the others (Osborne 1995).

Perhaps the most important difference between Tai culture and those of others in southern and eastern Asia concerns the status of women, which was and remains quite high in comparison. Tai culture contained a focus on the nuclear family with all members contributing labor to the family economic activity of subsistence agriculture. Social organization was based on villages of 10 to 30 families, and within a village labor was shared for tasks beyond the resources of individual families, such as harvesting and the completion of village projects. Governance was through an informal council of elders that coordinated village activities and resolved disputes. Small groups of 10 to 30 villages were organized into larger political entities called *muang* and governed by a *chao,* or lord of the muang. These larger political entities were formed out of the need for defense and for purposes of facilitating trade. Like much of Thai political organization in later times, the organizing principle of the muang was not territory but the relationship of the subsidiary villages to the chao of the leading village.

In terms of religious beliefs the Tai were **animists** who viewed the world as inhabited by many spirits, both good and bad. Ceremonies and offerings propitiated these spirits to prevent harm or incur favor. Another important and continuing characteristic of Tai society was its personal nature. Relationships between people, both those between equals and those between superiors and subordinates, were personal and based on mutual obligations between individuals (Wyatt 1984: chap. 1). This personal nature of Thai society, as we have already seen, remains to this day and is crucial in understanding contemporary Thailand.

Although the original Tai comprise the single largest group in contemporary Thailand, the kingdom's population is actually a heterogeneous mixture of several Asian peoples. As we shall see, some groups, especially the Chinese, came to Thailand in pursuit of trade and economic opportunity, while others were incorporated into the kingdom through the long history of conflict with neighboring countries. Compared to eastern and southern Asia, the southeast was relatively underpopulated until the 20th century, and Thailand's history is one of virtually continuous warfare until the early 19th century. During the many wars with the Burmese and Khmer (Cambodians), the Tai took slaves when victorious and similarly were enslaved when conquered. As late as the 1840s, the Thai monarchy was settling Lao, Malay, Vietnamese, and Khmer captives in the kingdom (Wyatt 1984; Osborne 1995). Additionally, the relative peace and prosperity in Thailand compared to neighboring countries caused substantial numbers of Mons and Burmese to settle there. These immigrants have been largely integrated into contemporary Thai society through marriage and acculturation. To be a Thai citizen today means to speak the standard or central Thai language and adhere to Thai customs and culture, but it does not mean one is distinctively Tai in an ethnic sense. Even the royal family has Chinese and other nationalities in its lineage.

A HISTORY OF THE THAI KINGDOMS

The following dates of the early Thai kingdoms will be useful to remember as we move through the history of early Thailand:

> Sukothai, A.D. 1253–1350
>
> Ayudhya, A.D. 1350–1767
>
> Thonburi, A.D. 1767–1782
>
> Bangkok, 1782–present

Sukothai, 1253–1350

The nation known today as Thailand traces it history through the major Thai kingdoms established from the middle of the 13th century onward in the central plain of the Chao Phaya River basin. Sukothai, originally a

regional capital of the Khmer empire, is viewed as the first true Thai
kingdom as it was the first to unite a considerable number of muang,
control an extensive territory, and most important, receive international
recognition through a formal tributary status with China, the super-
power of the day in Asia. As noted in beginning this chapter, the city of
Sukothai exists to this day, and the ruins of this ancient capital can be
easily visited by bus or train from Bangkok. The size and scope seem
modest in comparison to contemporary cities; but walking through the
ruins, brick walls in various states of disrepair, the foundations outlining
buildings, streets, and squares, one gets some sense of life in the kingdom. Among the many aspects of Sukothai that are of relevance to understanding modern Thailand is that its economic base was an adequate
food supply and that it served as a center of regional trade.

The relationship between religion and politics that persists to the
present was also established in Sukothai. Kingship in Sukothai is best described as patriarchy. During war the king was a military leader, and in
time of peace he was a father figure who was expected to provide advice
and judgment in all matters and whose decisions were accepted by the
people. That the king maintained fairly close relationships with the populace is evidenced by the fact that a gong was hung outside the palace.
When people needed the king's service, say to settle disputes or give advice, they could summon him by ringing this gong (Akin 1996: 25). The
monarch also had the role and responsibility of protector and promoter
of Buddhism, which provided the moral foundation of society, though at
the same time animism, the traditional form of religion, was recognized
and respected. In all of Southeast Asia, the idea that the world of humans
should reflect the nature and organization of the metaphysical world, the
world of the gods, was prevalent, and the position of the king as a wise,
powerful, and approachable ruler was a representation of a Buddhist
form of this belief (Keyes 1989: 32; Akin 1996: 25).

Beyond these basic facts little is known of the social organization
of Sukothai or the details of life in the kingdom. It is known that the
political organization of Sukothai was **feudal-estate system,** or **feudalism,** an extension of the personal relationships of traditional Tai social
organization. At the center was the king; in a chain of submission
below the king, the rulers or lords of major principalities (muang) sub-
mitted directly to him, and through allegiance to these lords subsidiary
units owed indirect allegiance to the king. Since the allegiances to the
king were not formal legal relationships between political entities but
temporary personal relationships between individual rulers, the system
did not provide the stability, authority, and control necessary to sustain
the kingdom. When either of the parties to the relationship died, the
ruler of a principality or the king, the personal relationship was sev-
ered and it was up to the successors to reestablish it if desired and possible. Although the system of a structure of submission and allegiance
between independent rulers was similar to European feudalism, there

was an important difference. In the Thai system the king, at least in theory, owned all land and subordinate rulers had no inherent rights to the lands they governed.

Although lasting but a century, the Sukothai kingdom began the process that eventuated in the modern nation we know as Thailand. Certainly in Thailand the achievements of Sukothai are recognized, even reified. Among the kingdom's achievements, its great king Ramkamheng (1279?–99?) is claimed to have devised the first writing system for a Thai language, and Sukothai was definitely a center of Buddhist art and culture under the patronage of the kings (Keyes 1989: 25). There is the famous description of Sukothai on a stone lintel found at the site of the city's ruins, perhaps provided by Ramkamheng himself. While there is some dispute as to the authenticity of the lintel, its contents provide insight into contemporary Thai society:

> There is fish in the water and rice in the fields . . . . [and after emphasizing the ability of all to trade] When commoners or men of rank differ and disagree, the King examines the case to get at the truth and then settles it justly for them . . . [after emphasizing the king's honesty] If any commoner in the land has a grievance that sickens his belly and gripes his heart, and which he wants to make known to his ruler and lord, it is easy; he goes and strikes the bell which the King has hung there; King Ramkamheng . . . hears the call . . ., examines the case and decides it justly for him. (Wyatt 1984: 54)

Even today Thais commonly describe their country as one with fish in the water and rice in the fields, a land of plenty, and certainly they look to the king for wisdom and justice.

Ayudhya, 1350–1767

Sukothai had two serious disadvantages that prevented long-term success. The feudal system made the kingdom politically weak, and despite being a center of trade, it was not located on a major river. Ayudhya is located to the south of Sukothai on the Chao Phaya river in a much more advantageous position than Sukothai for communication and trade. Like Sukothai the ruins of this ancient capital can be visited conveniently today from Bangkok. However, since the city was sacked by the Burmese in 1767 and much of the treasure removed to Burma, and then later much of the remaining material was shipped to Bangkok for construction of the new capital or stolen for museums and sale in the West, only the vestiges of the ancient city are left (Osborne 1995). With respect to knowledge of society and politics, though, much more is known about Ayudhya than Sukothai. And we know that most important in Ayudhya were the changes in political and social organization designed to increase the kingdom's political strength and security. Ayudhya faced the established empire of the Khmer (from today's Cambodia) to the east, Burma to the west, and competing Thai kingdoms to the north. There is a historical continuity from the earlier Thai who had not developed political systems for governing large areas of territory with numerous subunits (what would constitute a kingdom in the political world of Southeast Asia); to the first attempt to do so at Sukothai, which was short lived; to Ayudhya, which survived and flourished for centuries (Wyatt 1984).

A key element of the political change that made this success possible was the adoption of the Khmer and Burmese organizational models, which had demonstrated success in those countries. The first and most important task was to strengthen the power, legitimacy, and authority of the king (remember this was a relatively new institution in Thai society) in relationship to the hereditary nobility and local rulers and directly over commoners. Therefore, kingship was redefined so that the king was no longer the benevolent patriarch of Sukothai; instead, adopting a Hindu concept, the king would be divine, a god king. This change expanded and altered the Buddhist concept of the king as first among mortals and promoter and protector of religion with duties and responsibilities in the religious realm and toward the people; it put the king beyond criticism. In addition to many rituals affirming the divine status of the king, laws and regulations reinforced the new belief. No longer could common people summon the king with a gong to hear their petitions but instead they were subjected to lashes with a whip before their petitions

A veiw of one of the old capitals, Sukothai (1253–1350), as it exists today in north central Thailand.

were forwarded. Common people were forbidden to look at the king or touch any member of the royal family under penalty of death, and even nobles had to approach the king by crawling on their hands and knees.

Another adoption from the Khmer and Burmese models was a formal structure of government administrative departments. Under this "household system" the king appointed the heads of the ministries, usually from the hereditary nobility or royal family, and the appointed individual then fulfilled the responsibilities of office by use of personal resources. The ministries were literally run out of the ministers' homes or palaces. Each ministry was like a subgovernment performing multiple functions such as collecting taxes, raising armies, constructing public works, and administering justice in their region of responsibility in the kingdom. The ministers were directly accountable to the king, a sort of kingly bureaucracy, and the king could focus on managing the local rulers and maintaining their allegiance.

The main purpose of the new structure of governance was to gain control of revenue and, even more important, manpower. The entire society was therefore organized in a hierarchical military fashion. The largest units were *krom,* the larger of which, such as the household departments described above, were equivalent to military divisions; the smaller and more specialized were equivalent to regiments. Each krom was further subdivided into *kong,* the equivalent of battalions, and *mu,* the equivalent of platoons. Every male within the kingdom was assigned a position within this organizational structure from which they could be compelled to serve as soldiers in time of war or perform the annual **corvee,** required unpaid labor for the king (Akin 1996: 31). A most notable feature of life in Ayudhya was the constant struggle of common people to avoid the hated corvee while the king was consistently promulgating regulations to prevent the movement of common people into the ranks of the nobility and enforce the labor requirement. Nobles and princes could increase their popularity, power, and wealth by building a clientele protected from the requirements of the corvee. It may be that the extreme significance of informal patron-client networks in Thai society was greatly strengthened by this structure and process. In times of war or for the completion of public projects, the local leadership calculated the costs and risks of acceding to the king's requests against the benefits. Frequently the calculation resulted in a conclusion that it was not in the best interest of the local ruler to comply with the king's demands (Akin 1996).

Despite the adoption of the Hindu concept of the god king and the theory that the king was an absolute ruler with all authority and power, the reality was quite different. Politics, in terms of conflict over the kingship and control of the resources of government, was constant but most pronounced when a king died and a successor had to be chosen (Wyatt 1984). A king could express a preference about who would succeed to the throne, but the kingdom had no law of succession, such as primogeniture in Europe where the monarch's sons in order from oldest to youngest had claim to the throne. Upon the death of a king a council composed of the heads of the major krom, leading nobles and princes, and the patriarchs at the head of the Buddhist monkhood would meet to decide upon a successor. During these councils the informal networks of patrons and clients came into play as those with a claim to the throne attempted to influence the council in its selection. Because these Thai kings practiced polygamy and brothers and sons were both eligible for succession, there were always a large number of potential claimants to the throne. In almost every instance of succession there was conflict, and it frequently took several years to settle the claims, creating a period during which the kingdom was substantially weakened. The final Burmese conquest of Ayudhya in 1767 came at a time when factionalism had gotten beyond the control of the king, and forces could not be mobilized for the defense of the kingdom.

Thonburi, 1767–1782

The significance of the brief Thonburi period is that it reestablished the Thai kingdom that had been destroyed by the Burmese with the fall of Ayudhya. The Thai resurgence was due in large part to the leadership of the former governor of Tak, a province of Ayudhya. Now known as Taksin (Tak the great), he had fled Ayudhya with his soldiers when its defense became hopeless. Having survived the Burmese conquest, he later conducted a series of military campaigns that both expelled the Burmese and brought the Thai kingdoms back under central control. He established a new capital at Thonburi on the west side of the Chao Phaya River, across from what is today Bangkok.

Despite these successes, Taksin's reign and the Thonburi period were very brief due to political and personal factors. Taksin was not a member of the old ruling elite of Ayudhya and never fully accepted by that elite. He gave them an opportunity to act when he became convinced that he had progressed to the stage where in seven more reincarnations he would become a Buddha. While this in itself would not have served to generate opposition, and might in fact have worked to his advantage, he violated the cardinal Buddhist principle of showing respect to all monks by insisting that all, including the leaders of the monkhood, publicly pay him respect. When the monks who refused were punished, the old elite from Ayudhya decided that Taksin needed to be removed. They agreed that one of the leading generals, a member of one of the old Ayudhya ruling families, a Chakri, should take the throne. In ritual fashion, King Taksin was wrapped in a robe and beaten to death with a sandalwood club, the new king was crowned, and the Chakri dynasty begun.

Early Bangkok Period, 1782–1932

The defeat at the hands of the Burmese worked to the advantage of the new dynasty. During the war with Burma, many of the potential challengers with a claim to the throne had been killed. Defeat had also forced the elite of Thai society to realize that unity was essential to ensure the survival of the nation and their position in it. Thus, the new king had a free hand in the appointment of senior ministers and was able to assure their loyalty by naming family and other supporters to all high-level positions. The king's authority was further strengthened by reemphasizing the Buddhist version of kingship from Sukothai. While Thai society remained organized much as it had in Ayudhya, the crisis of the Burmese conquest had, at least temporarily, greatly increased the power and control of the monarchy.

The first tests of these reforms were several Burmese attempts at conquest, which were successfully fended off. Not only were the Burmese attacks defeated, but the kingdom was able to extend its borders to more than twice the size of the kingdom of Ayudhya. Eventually, in addition to the territory of Ayudhya, the kingdom covered all of present day Laos, the eastern provinces of Cambodia, with Cambodia itself a tributary state, and several provinces on the Malay peninsula.

Just as this great new Thai kingdom established itself, a new and more dangerous challenge to the kingdom than it had previously faced came to dominate its concerns. The new threat was, of course, Western imperialism. Thailand had long had relations with several Western countries, sending its first diplomatic delegations in the early 17th century, and it had always dealt with these Europeans as equals. Now, with the Europeans' increased power, the kingdom would have to deal with France and Britain as potentially dangerous adversaries.

As the kingdom was reestablishing itself and then expanding, the British and the French began to extend their colonial empires into Southeast Asia, closing in on Thailand from all sides. During the period from the 1820s through the 1860s, Britain established colonial domination of Burma and the Malay peninsula, putting the British on Thailand's western and southern borders. At the same time, France established a colonial presence in Vietnam, Laos, and Cambodia, placing Thailand under pressure on its eastern and northern borders. The threat posed by the European powers was described in the 1860s by King Monkut (Rama IV) as a choice between swimming up river to make friends with the crocodile or swimming out to sea hanging on to the whale, referring to the French and British, respectively. It was King Monkut and his son King Chulalongkorn (Rama V) who astutely lead the nation during the most crucial period of confrontation with the West from the 1850s until the turn of the century—a period in which the kingdom began its transformation into a modern nation-state. During this period the Western powers, and Britain in particular, greatly limited the freedom of action of the Thai elites and forced the integration of Thailand into the economic system dominated by the West (Chaiyan 1994).

The reaction to the threat from Western powers has come to be called *bamboo diplomacy* in Thailand, in reference to how bamboo survives violent tropical storms by bending but not breaking. With regard to Thai policy toward the British and French, the bending was in the form of concessions necessary to achieve the overriding goal, that which could not be broken: national independence from foreign rule.

The first type of concession was the acceptance of unequal treaties, the first of which was negotiated with Britain in 1855, followed by similar agreements with other Western nations, including France and the United States. Under the terms of these treaties Thailand accepted Western terms of trade, including low limits on taxes from imports and exports, the right of foreigners to own property in the kingdom, and extraterritorial rights. Extraterritorial rights meant that a foreign national from countries with such treaties had the right to have legal disputes arising under Thai law tried in courts established by their home country. This, and the other provisions of the treaties, clearly represented a loss of national sovereignty on the part of the kingdom, but at least Thai rule over Thai subjects was retained.

The second type of concession was territorial. Between 1867 and 1909 the kingdom accepted the loss of territory to Britain and France equivalent to half the territory it held at the beginning of the era of confrontation. France gained control over all of present-day Laos and Cambodia, and Britain gained control over several provinces on the Malay peninsula. Thailand was reduced to essentially the old territory of Ayudhya.

The alternatives available to Thailand at this time were extremely limited. No country in Southeast Asia and none in East Asia, except Japan, escaped Western domination during this era as the differential in economic and military power between the Western countries and those in Asia was so great. Thailand had the evidence of the fate of the other Asian nations before it, saw the inevitable result of stubborn resistance, and made the wise decision to follow the path of flexibility and accommodation.

In addition to making concessions the kingdom also developed a more assertive policy of multilateralism. Accepting the fact of the power of the Western nations, Thailand attempted, quite successfully, to balance the influence of the various Western powers against each other, although Great Britain, the first of the Western nations to sign an unequal treaty, was clearly the most influential. Overall, Thai policy in this period was quite successful considering the circumstances. The kingdom did retain its independence and developed along its own lines under pressure from, but not subjugation to, a European power.

The effects of the struggle to avoid colonization occurred in several areas. The government lost substantial revenues from the loss of taxes and trading monopolies and substituted internal monopolies in gambling, alcohol, a national lottery, and opium. Although these sources made up the lost revenue, they also directly involved the government in socially destructive economic activity, especially the opium trade. A more general and significant economic impact was that the privileged position of the Western nations prevented the development of industry in the kingdom because the Western powers' purpose of the treaties was to maintain the kingdom as a source of raw materials for themselves and a market for their manufactured products.

In the political and social realm, the response of the Thai monarchy was to combat the nation's relative weakness by beginning to transform the kingdom into a modern nation-state. Initially the sons of the elite, and later commoners, were sent abroad to acquire Western education and expertise, as was done by the Japanese at about the same time. Under the leadership of King Chulalongkorn, the government administration was transformed from the old household system to a modern bureaucratic form in which the civil servants worked for the king. In addition, a modern and permanent military force was established. In the early 1900s the corvee system and slavery were also abolished, and over time selected Western cultural practices were introduced to the population. In essence, much like in Japan at the same time (Kerbo and McKinstry 1998), the confrontation with the West stimulated the creation of the modern nation-state of Thailand.

The changes that occurred from the late 1800s into the early years of the 20th century, again as in Japan, were essentially a transformation from above directed by the monarchy and traditional elites. The conflict between the monarchy and the hereditary elite was resolved in favor of the monarchy, and the rigidly organized social hierarchy inherited from Ayudhya was abandoned. What is most important to note is that these changes, emanating from the confrontation with the West, occurred in a society in which the social structure and norms had remained stable for centuries. The response to the challenge of the West created new sources of power in society, which in turn led to instability. For example, as the peasants lost the traditional power of local patrons and became subject to the direct control of the central government, as with the head tax that had replaced the corvee, the new system created hardships from which there was no protection. Thus, in the early 1900s, for the first time Thailand experienced a new form of rebellion in peasant-based attempts to resist the new central authority of the monarchy. In response to these pressures, in 1912 a group of junior military officers planned a coup to overthrow the monarchy. Poorly planned and without much support, the coup plot was discovered and the instigators punished. But the peasant rebellions and the attempted coup demonstrated that monarchical rule was under challenge.

In the early 1930s, as the effects of the worldwide economic depression were felt in Thailand, the government's response was ineffectual; and the tensions brought on by confrontation with the West and the creation of a more modern nation-state came to the crisis point. Most affected were the small middle class, government civil servants, military officers, and a small urban commercial group. As all government employees had their salaries cut and taxes increased, while the king and royal family retained power and a luxurious standard of living, resentment grew. Finally in June 1932, the "promoters," as they called themselves (49 military officers and 65 civilians, most educated in the West), staged a coup. The promoters, having accepted the Western value that ability and achievement should be the criteria for leadership and positions of authority were motivated by the conviction that the absolute monarchy was an obstacle to the modernization and development of Thailand. They were also convinced that a Western model of government was necessary for the kingdom. The 1932 coup set the pattern for this type of event in Thailand as it was very well planned and resulted in little violence. In the highly centralized system created under the monarchy's control of key military forces, control over the centers of government in Bangkok meant control of the country. The king, vacationing at the seaside, agreed to a request from the conspirators that he abdicate; thus, centuries of rule under a system of absolute monarchy came to an end.

Late Bangkok Period, 1932–Present

Although the overthrow of the absolute monarchy is referred to as "the revolution," it is important to distinguish between a **coup** and **revolution.** In a coup, those in political authority change but, unlike a revolution, there is very little change in the wider society or economy. In the short run, the events of 1932 were a coup, and in terms of daily life most Thais were completely unaffected. The promoters were not representatives of a mass-based political movement and had to attempt to create one after the fact of the successful coup. However, in the long term the abolition of absolute monarchy in 1932 marked the beginning of a revolution since it initiated changes that in the post–World War II era would lead to the transformation of Thailand from a traditional Asian kingdom into a modern and dynamic nation.

What unified the coup plotters was only the conviction that absolute monarchy had to end. The promoters comprised three groups: A civilian faction advocating radical social and economic change; a group of junior military officers greatly opposed to the monarchy and extremely nationalistic; and a group of senior military officers who wished to end the inefficiencies of the monarchy but maintain it as a significant institution. The promoters needed to provide both the populace and the

Western nations, which might have intervened if they felt their interests were threatened, with some justification for the coup. The promoters, therefore justified their actions as a move to establish a democratic form of government in the kingdom. Of course, the kingdom had absolutely no experience of democracy, a basically illiterate peasant population, and the military contingent of the promoters with no commitment to real democracy.

The promoters' justification of the coup under the guise of democracy set the stage for a period in Thai history where the country often had the form of democratic government but not the substance. Between 1932 and 1938, first the civilian faction and then the senior military officers lost in the struggle to control the new government. It was the middle-level nationalistic and antimonarchical military officers among the original promoters, particularly the army, who dominated the government in alliance with civilian officials in the bureaucracy. The trappings of democracy in the form of a constitution and a parliament were maintained, in line with democratic justification of the original coup, while Thailand was actually governed by the military. This pattern continued with deviation for direct military dictatorship until 1973 (Wyatt 1984, Prudhisan 1992).

The leader of the military bureaucratic alliance that came to control the Thai government was Pibul Songkram, who had been a major at the time of the coup. He and his colleagues, like many Asian nationalists at the time, found in the military-dominated government of Japan an alternative to the Western democratic model of government that promised a means of achieving equality with the West. Following the Japanese model, the Pibul government promoted the role of the military, authoritarian government, and Thai nationalism, which included changing the formal name of the country from Siam to Thailand.

The imitation of Japan and the onset of World War II created an extremely peculiar situation for Thailand. Following the Japanese attack on Pearl Harbor on December 7, 1941, the Japanese attacked Thailand, and Thai troops briefly resisted before Pibul agreed to an armistice and then joined in alliance with Japan, followed by declarations of war against the United States and the allies. Pibul was convinced the Japanese would defeat the United States and thought the war supplied the opportunity to apply the Japanese model more thoroughly in Thailand (Prudihsan 1992). Other Thais, including the ambassador to the United States, assessed the situation differently, were confident of ultimate American success, and found more to emulate in a democratic model of government and development. The ambassador refused to deliver the Thai declaration of war and the U.S. government refused to recognize it so that, technically, a state of war never existed between the United States and Thailand.

A "Free Thai" movement, supported by the United States, was organized to oppose the Japanese occupation and to assist the Allied war effort. This movement gained strength as the war progressed and it became clear that Japan would lose the war in the Pacific, and in 1944 Pibul was removed as head of the Thai government. Not only was Japan's imminent defeat apparent, but during this period Thailand suffered as the rice and other materials originally sold to the Japanese were expropriated by them, and Bangkok was bombed by the Allies. When the war was over Thai leaders recognized the preeminent power of the United States, which replaced Britain as the most influential Western nation in Thailand. The wartime links between the Free Thai movement and the United States helped Thailand escape the worst of the consequences of officially supporting Japan.

Early in the war Thailand had by force reclaimed portions of Cambodia, Laos, and the Malay peninsula, ceded to France and Britain under pressure during the struggle to avoid colonization. Britain and France insisted that Thailand be treated as an enemy country, subjected to an occupation government and forced to pay war reparations. With the Thai government now dominated by the Free Thai supporters, the United States intervened on Thailand's behalf, the reclaimed lands were returned to Britain and France, and only minimal reparation requirements were established. Incredibly, in a unique series of events, Thailand escaped the war, its alliance with Japan, and the postwar conflicts with Britain and France relatively unharmed.

Thailand and the Cold War

The post–World War II international environment facing Thailand was, again, characterized by insecurity. With the onset of a communist-led revolution against the French in Vietnam in 1946 and the success of the communist revolution in China in 1949, Thailand was soon drawn into the Cold War. Postwar Thai governments were decidedly anticommunist and established a close and strong alliance with the United States, leading some Thais to refer to this as the "American Era" of Thai history. Thailand sent troops to participate in the United Nations forces fighting in Korea in the early 1950s and, in the 1960s and 70s, to Vietnam during the American war against the communist forces there. The American withdrawal from Vietnam and Southeast Asia in the mid-1970s combined with U.S. rapprochement with China created an extremely difficult situation for Thailand.

The success of the communist government of North Vietnam in unifying that country was accompanied by the victory of the communist Khmer Rouge in Cambodia and Pathet Lao in Laos. Thailand then had hostile communist forces on its entire eastern border and substantial portions of the north. The situation worsened when Vietnam, with what was then the world's fourth largest military, invaded and occupied Cambodia in 1978, placing Vietnamese troops on the Thai border. (A glance at the map of Southeast Asia will show you what a short distance it is from the Cambodian border to Bangkok.) Vietnam also explicitly articulated the idea of a Southeast Asian federation under its domination.

In this extremely threatening situation, Thailand, like the United States and China, supported the Khmer Rouge resistance to the Vietnamese occupation of Cambodia. The tension persisted throughout the 1980s as Thailand was forced to contend with real threats on both the Cambodian and Laotian borders where there were considerable conflict and incursions by hostile troops. The situation finally improved in 1989 with a UN-negotiated withdrawal of Vietnamese forces from Cambodia as the Soviet support that Vietnam relied upon collapsed and the poor performance of the Vietnamese economy created sufficient pressure.

From the mid-19th century into the early 20th century, Thailand had to fend off the global force of European imperialism. The Cold War era was one in which Thailand, still a small and relatively weak country, had to contend with the global conflict of communism versus the Western democracies. This conflict was driven by the politics and strategy of the superpowers, the United States and the Soviet Union. Again, remarkably, like the bamboo, Thailand weathered the storm of the Cold War and successfully negotiated its way through this challenging era by focusing on its primary goal of maintaining national independence and adapting to the international situation in pursuit of that goal. While this often meant close adherence to American interests, the Thais on occasion did follow independent policies as it suited their interests, particularly with regard to China. The success of Thailand surviving the wars that ravaged Southeast Asia during the Cold War era is even more remarkable, particularly when seen in the context of contending with and defeating a domestic communist insurgency as well. Additionally, during the period of conflict from the early 1960s through the 1980s, Thailand managed to achieve significant levels of economic growth, and during the 1980s the growth rates were among the highest in the world, with export trade playing a significant role.

INTERPRETING THAI HISTORY

The review of Thai history presented above provides a broad outline and some information significant to the creation of the contemporary Thai nation-state. What the review does not explore is the fundamental question of the nature of Thai society in terms of power relationships and their significance. This is an important topic that is part of the current question of Thai identity: What does it mean to be Thai? Thai history originally was court history, where chronicles of each king's reign were produced under royal auspices. After the coup of 1932 the history of kings was modified to include the idea of the nation-state to legitimize a new political order without an absolute monarchy. As they have for more than 500 years, however, the monarchy and the *sangha* (higher Buddhist priesthood) still form the basis for the legitimacy of the government.

Western scholarship on Thai history has focused on its uniqueness from the rest of Asia, the relative well-being of the peasantry, the escape from colonialism, the lack of radical revolutionary movements, and the consequent indigenous and organic development of Thai society. The court histories produced under royal auspices did not, of course, contain any criticisms of the kings, instead portraying them as benign, wise, and always acting in the best interests of the Thai nation and people. They also emphasized the importance of the role of the court in Bangkok as the primary determinant of Thai historical development, ignoring the role of more ordinary people and regional cities.

There are other perspectives. Beginning in the 1950s a few Thai scholars began to articulate the view that a society based on the authority of the monarchy and sangha was repressive and exploitive of the Thai people (Reynolds 1987; Chaiyan 1994). Questions were raised: Are Buddhism and the monarchy used to protect and satisfy the interests and goals of an elite, and are those interests congruent with the interests of the vast majority of citizens? In this regard the question of Thai identity revolves around the individual's relationship to authority, the monarchy and Buddhism in the form of the sangha. Should individuals accept this authority? To what degree? Do citizens have rights in opposition to these sources of authority and power? We will return to these questions in subsequent chapters as we examine the characteristics and dynamics of Thai society.

CONCLUSION

We are now primarily finished with our broad sweep of the history of Thailand and the history of the world that has affected Thailand. And in doing so, it is useful to put it all into the perspective of the present.

A number of movies about wars and conflicts in Southeast Asia in recent years have included some coverage of Thailand, but usually only brief coverage. Revolutions in Vietnam, Cambodia, Indonesia, and repressive dictatorships in places like Burma make for more dramatic movie plots. When Thailand is depicted in these movies, there is often a common image presented, as in the movie *Killing Field*. Toward the end of this movie the main character is shown finally escaping the years of slaughter by the communist Khmer Rouge that left one million or more Cambodians dead. Then comes the dramatic scene: As he emerges from the jungle into a clearing, there in the distance is the Thai border, a haven for refugees from many of Thailand's neighboring nations.

Despite the many social problems, relative subversion of democracy, and difficult conditions for many Thai people, we must acknowledge that during the horrors of the 20th century, a century in the world and in the region that has proven to be the most bloody in the whole history of human societies, Thailand stands out as a relative sea of tranquility and prosperity. It is understandable how that Thai border looks so inviting to so many people in the region.

We turn now to a closer look at the basic social institutions in Thailand, those that have shaped and molded the people and their activities, that have produced the successes of the Thai people as well as their social problems. Our goal is to demonstrate the relationship of these institutions to Thai development and failure, to the shaping of contemporary society, and how it is that the kingdom was able to remain a relative sea of tranquility among its neighbors in Asia.

CHAPTER 3

The Thai Economy, Economic Development, and the Modern World System

Compared to other nations in the region, the relative tranquility and social order in Thailand during the 20th century, as noted in ending our last chapter, has been remarkable. But almost as remarkable has been Thailand's rapid economic development. Yes, during the late 1990s Thailand experienced economic problems with a rapid decline in their real estate market and stock market and a severe decline in the value of their currency, the Thai baht. But when we consider how soon Thailand had begun to recover from these economic problems by the end of 1999, and especially when we consider where the Thai economy was only 25 years ago, Thai economic development remains impressive. As we will discuss later in this chapter, the economic setbacks of the late 1990s might best be referred to as growing pains.

Because of their economic power and rapid development, South Korea, Taiwan, Singapore, and Hong Kong have long been referred to as the "Asian tigers" (Vogel 1991). Beginning in the 1980s, Thailand was commonly referred to as the "fifth tiger" (Muscat 1994). For many years in a row, Thailand's economy had growth figures in the double digits, figures almost unheard of in earlier times. The new wealth of Thailand's middle class has been truly impressive; the number of cars on the streets of Bangkok has been increasing at a rate of 20,000 per month during many years in the 1980s and 1990s. Indeed, one of Thailand's central problems has been the traffic and pollution caused by such rapid economic success.

In striking contrast to the situations in many developing countries, however, in Thailand the benefits have not simply gone to the rich and middle class; the poor have also benefited. Along with the other businesses, athletic shoe factories have been coming to Thailand for the cheap labor. But in contrast to most other developing countries, the unskilled laborers in Thailand have been receiving long-term benefits from such foreign investment. Until very recently, wages have been moving up and, perhaps the most important indicator of improved conditions for the masses, the poverty rate has been dropping rapidly. Just 30 years ago, almost 50 percent of Thais fell below a poverty rate measured on the basis of the cost of basic necessities. By the end of the 1990s, only 11 percent of Thai people fell below that measure of poverty (Pasuk and Baker 1998, 1996a).

As we will see in a later chapter, income inequality finally started to increase rapidly in the 1990s in Thailand. But this increase in inequality, in contrast to most other developing nations, occurred not because the rich were getting richer and the poor poorer, but because the rich and middle class were gaining faster than those at the bottom (Pasuk and Baker 1998, 1996a). Most important though, the bottom was at least coming up (Pranee 1995).

A basic subject of this chapter is how the Thai economy has achieved what seems impossible to people in many developing countries. We will begin by considering a brief history of the Thai economy, then turn to some of the most important characteristics of the economy in recent decades, both the good and bad aspects. Once these descriptions of the Thai economy, past and present, have been presented, we will move to the important topics of the modern world system, the difficulty for poorer countries in raising their standard of living today, and how, in the face of many odds, Thailand has achieved such dramatic economic development. We will end this chapter by discussing the economic crisis that began in 1997 and Thailand's prospects for recovery. But before taking up these subjects we must take a small detour to examine what are called basic institutions to better understand the subjects of several remaining chapters in this book.

SOCIAL INSTITUTIONS

All societies have developed what sociologists describe as **institutions** to deal with the most basic tasks that make life in human societies possible and in fact allow these societies to survive. For example, all societies must work out solutions to raising and socializing children, as well as taking care of personal needs of individuals, especially when they are old or ill. Societies have usually found it necessary to support and maintain organizations that help people explain where they came from and where they are going in the cosmos in order to make the mysterious and unknown somehow less frightening. All societies have also found it necessary to establish some type of leadership system to effectively identify and implement policies that will maintain the long-range health and stability of the society. And, of course, societies must work out solutions to obtaining basic necessities such as food, clothing, and shelter. These four general tasks have been referred to as *functional imperatives* (Parsons 1953). Without successful attention to these tasks, no society can survive over the long term.

In this chapter and the next, we will examine institutions that have evolved in the Thai society for dealing with two of these functional imperatives: adapting the environment to human need (the economy), and goal attainment (the political system). The options in dealing with these functional imperatives are many, and no society has established their institutions exactly like another society. Because of similar value systems, material conditions, and other historical traditions, of course, some societies have evolved roughly similar institutions. This is one reason we can broadly group many societies into the Western and Asian categories. Still, even within broad groupings of nations, there are differences and unique characteristics with respect to their institutional arrangements. As we have already pointed out, while the Thai society shares much with its Asian neighbors, there are some puzzling differences. And as we will see, some of these differences show up in the Thai economy.

THE THAI ECONOMY

Once outside of the central city of Bangkok, and away from the smaller cities of Chiang Mai and Hat Yai as well, what mostly catches the eye of a traveler is the lush shades of green in the farmland. It is often the coconut trees and palm trees of various kinds that stand out most. But also there are banana, mango, and other trees planted around farms or villages, producing delicious fruits not grown in Europe and North America. In the northcentral part of Thailand, the lush sugarcane fields catch the eye; in the far south it is rubber plantations. But almost everywhere there is the water, particularly water in the rice patties. At the right time of the year the traveler can see the beautiful rice patties with the young rice starting to grow, bright green all over the smooth pools of water. To add to the picture most Westerners have, of course, you need a peasant lady, equipped with a conical straw hat, bent over tending the rice, and water buffalo in other parts of the field. With over half of the Thai people still engaged in agriculture (Pasuk and Baker 1996b), all the ingredients for that picture remain in rural Thailand, except perhaps for the water buffalo, which are being replaced by the "iron buffalos" (small hand-driven tractors) because of increasing prosperity.

Thai Economic History

Throughout the centuries of Thai civilization, like most agrarian societies in Asia employing primarily wet rice agriculture, the household was the main production unit, while larger tasks such as irrigation were done on a communal or village level. But this form of social organization and the scenes from the countryside are changing rapidly.

It was during the period from the treaty with Britain in 1855 to the post–World War II era that the foundation for Thailand's contemporary economic development was set (Wyatt 1984). Still with a focus on agriculture, with increased resources that could be committed to drainage and irrigation projects, the amount of land under cultivation was greatly expanded. Additionally, new transportation networks, especially the railroads, opened new markets for agricultural produce. Large increases in agricultural production were also facilitated by the king's policy of promoting settlement of new rice lands by individual peasant households beginning in the 1870s.

These government policies were primarily intended to prevent the growth of a landlord class that could compete politically with the monarchy, but it had the effect of creating incentives to the peasants to increase production and also reduced the level of inequality in the countryside to a far greater extent than in most agrarian societies in either Asia or Europe. From the early 20th century, however, government policies to increase rice production promoted rural inequality again. In addition, the "green revolution" of the 1960s with new rice strains and modern agricultural techniques not only increased rice production but commercialized agriculture, requiring greater investments by farmers in seeds, fertilizers, and equipment, again resulting in more rural inequality (Pasuk and Baker 1996b).

An important point is that from 1870 to the immediate post–World War II period there was essentially no economic development in Thailand as **gross domestic product (GDP)** per capita remained constant (Sompop 1981). A 1939 Ministry of Commerce survey recorded only 445 industrial enterprises in the Bangkok area, and almost all had only a small number of employees (Hewison 1993). Thailand was one of the least developed countries in the world, and most analysts predicted that it would remain that way. But by the 1980s, World Bank statistics showed Thailand had the world's fastest growing economy (Pasuk and Baker 1996b: 367). The value of exports of medium-high-technology products in 1994 was 28 times greater than what it had been in 1985, and those in labor-intensive products in the low-technology sector increased in value over sevenfold.

The Thai Economy Today

In contrast to the scenes of the Thai countryside described earlier, a far different scene exists in the center of the Thai economy today, that is, in Bangkok. From a tall building in the center of Bangkok, as far as the eye can see (even on a relatively clear day without much smog) there is nothing but huge buildings, many in various stages of completion. During a

Bangkok—A view from the temple of dawn on the west side of the Chao Phaya River in Bangkok.
Across the river is the modern city of Bangkok as well as the spires of the Grand Palace.

CNN interview in 1996, the mayor of Bangkok reported some 4,000 new buildings being constructed at that time in the city. In addition to all of this, roads are in disarray, with new elevated highways and an elevated train being built to deal with the problem of thousands of new cars added to Bangkok streets every month. And ringing the city are many huge industrial parks with more than 100 new factories in each park, resulting in hundreds of big buses parked around each industrial park waiting to transport the thousands of workers home in the evening. It is obvious to anyone that Bangkok, and Thailand in general, has achieved a rapid stage of economic growth propelling the country and its people into massive changes.

These changes are reflected in the basic economic figures. In the 1960s, food, beverages, and tobacco accounted for over 60 percent of GDP. In 1970, food and beverages remained the two largest components, though textiles had moved into third place. In 1980, textiles moved into second place; but by the end of the 1980s, textiles had moved to first place, with finished garments and shoes to third behind food. By 1990, transportation equipment, machinery, electronic components, and fabric components had developed sizable shares in manufacturing GDP (Warr 1993; Falkus 1995; Muscat 1994).

Today Thailand has achieved substantial diversification and sophistication in industry. Japanese automakers such as Toyota, Nissan, Honda, and Isuzu have assembly and component manufacturing plants in Thailand. Ford is building an auto manufacturing plant just outside of Bangkok, and General Motors in 1996 began a $750 million project to build an assembly plant for pickup trucks southeast of Bangkok (both, unfortunately, too late to catch the biggest expansion of auto sales in Thailand). Many Japanese electronics companies have manufacturing facilities, as do some American companies such as American Micro Devices (AMD), which makes semiconductors. And Seagate, the American-based manufacturer of computer hard drives, is the single largest employer in Thailand.

The major changes in the Thai economy can be seen in Table 3–1. There are two major developments to be observed. First, there was growth in all sectors of the economy during the time period. Second, the most rapid growth was in manufacturing, which fundamentally changed the character of the Thai economy and society. Perhaps most striking are the figures in the bottom line, the overall growth in gross domestic product, the total of all goods and services produced per capita. Between 1960 and 1990 this figure increased by a factor of 12. (Given a relatively low cost of living, the figure of $1,200 for 1990 is somewhat misleading since it indicates a standard of living lower than is in fact the case.)

Other key developments illustrated in Table 3–1 are the relative decline of agriculture as a percentage of both GDP and exports, along with the rapid growth of the manufacturing sector. Changes in the percentage of the labor force employed by each sector demonstrate some of the problems regarding the development of the Thai economy. While the percentage of GDP attributable to manufacturing increased by 21 percent

TABLE 3-1

Industry Expansion in Thailand

	1960	1970	1980	1990
Agriculture, % GDP	39.8%	28.3%	23.2%	12.4%
Agriculture, % exports	90.5	70.3	58.3	22.6
Agriculture, % labor force	82.4	79.3	72.5	66.5
Industry, % GDP	18.2	25.3	28.4	39.2
Industry, % exports	1.0	15.0	32.0	63.0
Industry, % labor force	4.2	5.8	7.7	11.2
Services, % GDP	42.0	46.4	46.4	48.4
Services, % labor force	13.4	14.9	19.8	22.3
GDP per capita (constant 1990 dollars)	$100	$195	$688	$1,200
Annual growth rate		7.9%	6.9%	5.4%

Sources: Muscat 1994, Appendix, Table A2; Mehdi 1995, Table 2–1; Bank of Thailand, *Quarterly Bulletin*, various issues.

from 1960 to 1990, the proportion of the labor force employed in the sector increased by only 7 percent. Conversely, while the percentage of GDP attributed to the service sector increased by only 6.4 percent, the proportion of the labor force in services increased by 8.9 percent. In agriculture a 27.4 percent decline in contribution to GDP was accompanied by a 15.9 percent reduction in this sector's proportion of the labor force.

Finally, we can note the overall growth of the economy and the success of the export-driven growth are well illustrated in the change in the percentage composition of exports. Manufacturing's share increased from 1 to 63 percent over the time period. The pace of growth was exceptional, especially during the late 1980s and into the early 1990s, as demonstrated by the following and somewhat mind-numbing statistics: From 1980 to 1994 GDP increased in size over fourfold, with exports increasing sevenfold. The annual average growth rates were 7.6 percent for GDP and 14.3 percent for exports from 1980 to 1990 (World Development Report 1996).

The Underside of the Economic Miracle: Working in Thailand

The statistics and analysis presented above, with nearly miraculous growth and the vision of progress, however, obscure the underside of development. Despite the reduction of poverty noted earlier, the downside of the miracle is found especially in the informal economy but also in more general conditions for labor. In the informal economy, unlike the formal sector, workers do not work under personnel policies recognizing rights and obligations of employer and employee, workers are not protected by government regulation, and there is no security in work. Over half of the urban workforce is still in the informal sector (Nipon 1991).

We can use the case of the textile industry. In this industry, where shop owners may subcontract with retailers and exporters in ready-made garments, work hours are not fixed and often run from eight A.M. to midnight. Workers are paid on a piece work rate of about 20 to 30 cents per garment; shop owners can sell for double that price, with a final retail cost of at least 20 times what the worker receives. Most of these workers are women and teenagers, often sent to the city by their families in the countryside. Only 18 percent of these workers are covered by social security (*Bangkok Post*, November 23, 1996; Seagrave 1995).

In 1992 the Department of Labor Protection and Welfare inspected over 30,000 business establishments throughout the kingdom and found 70 percent to be in violation of labor laws. Of those establishments employing more than 1,000 persons, only 4 percent failed to pay the minimum wage although the overall rate of violation of regulations was 40 percent. Among businesses with 10–19 workers, 32 percent failed to pay the minimum wage, while among the smallest establishments the rate was 39 percent (Mathana and Pawadee 1994: 37).

It is important to stress, however, that it is not just in the informal sector that Thai workers are found with little protection and difficult working conditions. Unfortunately, the famous toy factory fire in May 1993 that killed nearly 200 workers and injured hundreds more is not untypical. The factory had no fire alarm or proper fire escapes, and factory construction was substandard. A nationwide check following the fire found that 60 percent of factories lacked fire alarms, 40 percent had no fire extinguishers, and almost as many had no emergency exits. Adding to this, there were a total of 50 inspectors responsible for enforcing fire regulations at 90,000 factories (Girling 1996: 78–79).

During the period of rapid economic development, government policy has been to limit, control, and at times ban labor unions. During a brief period of liberalization during 1973–76 there was some increased freedom for union organizing. More recently, however, the military leaders who briefly came to power in the coup of 1991 greatly reduced the influence of unions by (1) removing the legal rights of state workers to unionize and (2) weakening the laws regarding union rights in the private sector. As one might guess, overall the Thai union movement is weak and fragmented. Less than 5 percent of the workforce belongs to a union (Brown and Frenkel 1993: 88–89; Hewison 1993).

ECONOMIC DEVELOPMENT IN THAILAND AND THE MODERN WORLD SYSTEM

To understand the prospects or lack of prospects for growth among developing countries such as Thailand, we must briefly turn to another area of study within sociology, the **modern world system.**

For many years economists had assumed that all nations in the world would follow a similar pattern of economic development. With some initial capital investment, it was believed, nations would proceed on a path from preindustrial agrarian societies, like the very early history of today's industrial societies, to industrialization (see Rostow 1960). But we now know that these theories of economic development are highly misleading when applied to less developed nations today (Vogel 1991; Johnson 1982; Chase-Dunn 1975; Portes 1976). The realities faced by today's undeveloped and developing societies are far different from those faced by the already developed nations when they were in the process of economic development. There is now what has been called a modern world system with ranks among nations like an international classes system, which brings almost all nations under its effects (Wallerstein 1974, 1980, 1989; Chirot 1986; Kerbo 1996).

Among these new realities faced by poor nations today are fewer natural resources, a much larger population, and poorer climate (Myrdal 1970: 32–37). But often most important, the industrial nations of today did not have other developed nations to contend with during their early process of development. The result is that the less wealthy nations today find it much more difficult to achieve economic development (Thurow 1991).

While there is certainly variation among developing nations, especially in Asia as we will see, several studies have shown that even when less developed nations have extensive aid and investment from the rich nations such as the United States, these poorer nations have less long-term economic growth (Chase-Dunn 1989, 1975; Bornschier and Chase-Dunn 1985; Bornschier, Chase-Dunn, and Rubinson 1978; Snyder and Kick 1979; Stokes and Jaffee 1982; Nolan 1983). These poorer nations, of course, may have some economic growth for a few years because of the aid and investment coming from the rich countries. But the longer-term prospects for growth may actually be harmed by the kinds of outside aid and investment these poorer nations have received.

Although there are many reasons for these harmful economic effects, three reasons seem most important. The first involves a problem of structural distortion in the economy. For example, in a more normal economic process some natural resource, human or nonhuman, leads to a chain of economic activity. We can use the case of a core nation with extensive copper deposits. Mining the copper provides jobs and profits. The copper is then refined into metal, again providing some people with jobs and profits. The metal is then used by another firm to make consumer products, again providing jobs and profits. Finally, the products are sold by retail firms, again providing jobs and profits. From the mining process to the retail sales of the products, there is a chain of jobs and profits providing economic growth.

Now consider what may happen when the copper is mined in a poor nation with extensive ties to rich nations. The copper may be mined by native workers, but the ore or metal is usually shipped to rich nations where the remainder of the economic chain is completed. The additional jobs and profits from the chain of economic activities are lost to the developing nation—they go to corporations in the rich countries (Chase-Dunn 1975).

The second factor harming economic growth in poorer nations is related to political and economic power. When developing nations are heavily tied to multinational corporations from the rich nations, a small, wealthy elite that depends upon multinational corporations develops in the poor countries. This elite makes sure multinational corporations are happy with the relationship. The multinationals are allowed extensive tax breaks, and they are allowed to take most of the profits out of the country; in addition, wages to domestic workers are kept low. All this is likely to keep multinational corporations in the poor nation and, consequently, the small elite wealthy. But long-term economic growth is harmed. Profits go to the core and the very low wages paid to workers leave them with no buying power to stimulate the domestic economy.

The third negative effect on the economy of poorer nations is related to agricultural disruption. Export agriculture often becomes an important economic activity of a developing nation brought into the world economic system. Before this time traditional agriculture was directed toward local consumption, and there was no incentive to introduce capital-intensive methods of farming. As a result of traditional agricultural methods and lack of an extensive market for agricultural products, some land was left for poor peasants, food was cheaper, and jobs were more plentiful. But with export agriculture and capital-intensive farming methods, food becomes more expensive and poor peasants are doubly disadvantaged. They are ejected from the marginal land they previously farmed to increase the production of cash crops for the world market, and the more extensive use of machinery means there are fewer agricultural jobs. This also means exaggerated urbanization as peasants lose jobs and land, since they move to the cities in hopes of finding work there (Kentor 1981).

The above is not meant to suggest that all poor nations are equally hurt by investments from the rich nations, or are hurt in the same way.[4] But it is a common pattern, and we must consider how Thailand has been affected by its position in this modern world system and how its economic growth has been more extensive than found in most less developed nations.

The Rise of East and Southeast Asia: Exceptions That Fit the Rule

Traveling through East Asia and Southeast Asia it is difficult to miss the huge presence of multinational corporations from the rich nations. Walking through the streets of Seoul, Taipei, Bangkok, as well as the special economic zones of China (Vogel 1989), for example, one is impressed with the number of buildings displaying the logo of corporations from the United States, Japan, Germany, France, and a few others of the Western industrial powers. But walking through these cities one is also impressed with the massive economic development that has been in progress for sometimes two decades. The Seoul we visited in the late 1990s looked more like Tokyo in the early 1980s than the Seoul of 1950. Bangkok has grown more rapidly in the 1980s and early 1990s than did even Seoul or Tokyo before it.

The economic statistics strongly concur with these personal observations: With a few exceptions, these nations of East and Southeast Asia generally have the highest rates of economic growth in the world (Hill 1994). With rich nations in North America and Europe experiencing annual rates of 2 to 3 percent in good years, despite recent setbacks of the late 1990s, many of these Asian nations have been growing at 10 percent or more annually. So fast is the growth, the largest percentage of GNP for any single world region will soon be in this part of Asia.

The point of all this for our present discussion, of course, is that in contrast to the pattern for many if not most poor nations, outside investments from the rich nations not only do not harm these Asian economies such as Thailand but have been used for their long-term economic development. The discrepancies among developing nations presented by rapid development in Asia was first considered in an article titled "Dependency Theory and Taiwan: Analysis of a Deviant Case" (Barrett and Whyte 1982). Since this article appeared, it has become evident that there are other deviant cases, primarily in East and Southeast Asia (Hill 1994).

There are several common characteristics of these rapidly developing countries in Asia. Family ties and support for education are very strong, and a sense of group responsibility leads to more cooperation in work, education, and other sectors of the society. What can be described as a greater sense of responsibility on the part of many leaders (but certainly not all) is another factor cited by many people as a key to economic development in this region. It is in dispute whether or not it is the longer history of these nations, with relatively stronger traditions of responsibility for the citizens held by leaders, or the Asian religions, which restrain leaders and make them relatively more responsible to their citizens, or a mixture of both (Pye 1985). But it is clear that the artificial national boundaries created by colonialism in Latin America and Africa, and subsequently the newness of these nations, present leaders with fewer traditions of service and responsibility than the ancient civilizations of East and Southeast Asia.

Even more than this, however, it is the "hard state," or what has been called the **capitalist development state** with the case of Japan (Johnson 1982; Kerbo and McKinstry 1995), that is cited as being responsible for rapid and more even economic development in this part of the world (Vogel 1991; Hamilton and Biggart 1988; Numazaki 1991). It is a "hard state" with the interests of the whole nation in mind, a state able to make the tough decisions that must be made for economic planning and with the ability to carry out these decisions, that is often described as most important for their economic development (Vogel 1991; Pye 1985). It is a "hard state" within what is also called an Asian development model that includes extensive state intervention in the economy through ownership and economic planning. As we will see, Thailand's state has been less involved with economic planning compared to other Asian nations. But the Thai government over the years has passed many laws ensuring that outside investments are more likely to help rather than harm

Thailand's interests. For example, with some exceptions, if a foreign corporation wants to set up a factory in Thailand, it must form a joint venture with a Thai company, and 51 percent of ownership in the joint venture must be in the hands of Thai people. The exceptions, allowing wholly owned foreign enterprises or minority Thai participation, are designed to promote the transfer of higher levels of technology or encourage industries to locate in targeted development areas outside the congested Bangkok region. It is time that we consider this Asian development model and the case of Thailand in more detail.

The Asian Development Model and Thailand

Economic development bringing rising incomes, a large middle class, high standards of consumption, an educated population, and increases in health and life expectancy was primarily a Western phenomenon until the end of World War II. Japan had been something of an exception, but the outcome of World War II demonstrated that its productive capacity and level of technology were still far behind those of the West, particularly the United States. Since industrialization had first, and to that time only, occurred in the West, many scholars argued that the model of economic growth that had been followed by the West must be followed elsewhere (Johnson 1982; Bellah 1985). In the postwar era, however, this assumption was proven incorrect by the surprising resurgence of the Japanese economy and then by the emergence of what have come to be called the "dragon" or "tiger" economies of South Korea, Taiwan, Hong Kong, and Singapore.

The methods that led to these countries' rapid progress from agricultural to industrial economies were substantially different from the Western model and were identified as the Asian model of development (Vogel 1991). This Asian development model differs from that of the United States and the West most importantly by the level to which the government is involved in the economy with planning and even direct investments.

Like the four tigers and Japan, Confucian values also indirectly have had their place in furthering Thai economic development through its values emphasizing hard work, group cooperation or teamwork, and saving. Confucianism is not a part of the traditional Thai value system, but as noted in our beginning chapter, Thailand has a large ethnic Chinese community, concentrated in Bangkok, which has assumed a leading role in the business side of economic growth. Most of Thailand's leading corporations today were founded by Sino-Thai families who are still in control (Akira 1996; Wu and Wu 1980). In Thailand these ethnic Chinese own about 80 percent of private capital, along with 80 percent in Indonesia, 65 percent in Malaysia, and 40 percent in the Philippines (Hatch and Yamamura 1996: 82; Huntington 1996: 169).

An overall evaluation of Thailand's economic development, however, leads to the conclusion that in line with its history, the traditions of borrowing and learning from other cultures, Thailand has found its own way. To some extent this might also be predicted by the unique Thai value system and social organization described in our first chapter—a mix of Asian collectivism and somewhat Western individualism. But there have been other influences: Exposed to both the Japanese model and the example of the United States, Thailand has followed neither model exclusively, shifting emphasis over time and combining elements of both models. In contrast to the other successful economies of East Asia, Thailand has consistently placed less emphasis on the role of government as the director of development and instead emphasized the government's role as facilitator and supporter, but not director, of the private sector.

Thai Economic Development

The development of a modern economy in Thailand can be divided into four major periods. The period from 1932 until the mid-1950s was a period of economic nationalism; then from the 1950s into the 1970s the government primarily withdrew from economic involvement. But by the late-1970s to the mid-1980s the government again followed interventionist and protectionist policies. Finally, by the mid-1980s government policy was again oriented toward the market with emphasis on export-led growth. These periods can be further broken down to the period from the 1950s–70s when the kingdom followed a policy of **import substitution industrialization** (ISI) and then to the period from the mid-1980s when the policy switched to **export-oriented industrialization** (EOI). Throughout this section we will outline the changes these policies have brought to the Thai economy. But we must begin our description of the process of development by examining the foundation on which that growth was built.

Up from Poverty

The Thai economy did grow significantly during the period from 1870 to 1950, with growth derived from agricultural expansion while the population increased as well. Thailand's population was under 6 million in 1870, increasing to almost 20 million in 1950, but GDP per capita only increased from 973 to 1,138 baht (80 dollars, 1990 equivalent) during the same period (Sompop 1989; Muscat 1994). Thailand faced a problem many less developed nations face. Since population growth kept pace with economic growth, Thailand remained one of the poorest countries in the world, and its prospects for development looked dismal.

We have previously noted that the government created with the revolution of 1932 came to power without a mass base. As Thailand was a peasant nation, the government attempted to build its support in the peasantry in part by pursuing a policy of economic nationalism. Following the long Thai tradition of agricultural expansion, the export of agricultural products was used to generate the capital to finance industrial development. Under this strategy the government directed investment to industries that could produce products that previously had been available only through importation, the strategy of import substitution. These new industries were heavily protected by tariffs and, in the Thai case, were often state owned. The economic nationalism was in part a reaction to the unequal treaties imposed earlier by the West and was designed to make the country self-sufficient and economically independent. In line with this nationalist sentiment, the Chinese community in Bangkok was perceived as a threat to Thai identity and independence. The creation of state enterprises prevented the Chinese, who had capital and expertise, from becoming the dominant actors in the economy (see Muscat 1994 for the history of Thai economic development; for further interpretation and analysis, see Falkus 1995; Warr 1993; and Warr and Nidhiprabha 1996).

In general, economic nationalism and import substitution as economic policy are flawed. In the Thai case, the public enterprises were inefficient and poorly managed, and without competition there was no incentive to improve. Through time the existence of these state enterprises also provided a vehicle for corruption as the military-politicians in political control had shares freely issued to them, while losses of the enterprises were made up from the state budget. Often the same military officers established private companies, commonly run by their wives, which received exclusive state contracts, licenses, or monopoly privilege. Furthermore, the policy goal of limiting Chinese participation in the economy was also circumvented when military-politicians discovered they could use their positions to form joint ventures with Chinese bankers and businessmen. These businesses would then receive government financing, political protection, and often monopoly privilege while the government officials received free shares and places on the boards of directors. Although the system did produce new business enterprises, the accumulation and investment of capital, and some economic growth, it greatly limited the private sector in its flexibility and certainly did not allow market forces to drive the economy.

During 1957, two significant developments occurred: New political leadership was established when Marshall Sarit Thanarat staged a successful coup in 1958, and a World Bank advisory mission conducted a study of the Thai economy. In its 1959 report, the World Bank mission made two important recommendations that were subsequently adopted by the Sarit government. First, the report recommended that instead of investing in public enterprises (government-owned and -operated companies), it should instead invest in infrastructure development such as electricity generation and distribution, transportation, and communications.

The second recommendation was that the government should rely more on private investment, including foreign investment, to stimulate growth (Muscat 1994).

To facilitate investment, the National Economic and Social Development Board (NESDB) was created to produce regular development plans and the Board of Investment was set up to assist private investors. These changes met with approval from most of the business community, and unlike what has occurred in many developing countries, business leaders sought and obtained greater freedom from government rather than closer ties and protection.

The Sarit government initiated a new era of economic growth through increased agricultural exports. The stimulus of revenue from agricultural exports created domestic demand, which drove economic growth. This domestic demand accounted for the bulk of economic growth from 1966–78. From 1966–72, domestic demand accounted for 64 percent of industrial growth, which increased to 91 percent during 1972–75 and remained high at 80 percent from 1975–78. During the same three time periods, import substitution accounted for 29 percent of growth, then less than 1 percent, and finally –7.7 percent respectively (Falkus 1995). This initial phase of export-led growth set the foundation for Thailand's later industrialization. Despite the emphasis on agricultural exports, the proportion of GDP accounted for by industry increased substantially during the decade from 1960 to 1970, rising from under 19 percent to over 25 percent. This industrial growth supplied the domestic rather than the export market. During the same period the proportion of GDP derived from services also increased as the proportion from agriculture decreased.

By the early 1970s, economic growth based on agricultural export growth and the expansion of the domestic market had reached its limits. Agricultural growth had been achieved by increasing the amount of land under cultivation, but this process had reached its physical limits. South Korea, Taiwan, Singapore, and Hong Kong began their rush of economic growth by encouraging foreign investment, which was attracted by cheap labor, with the new production destined for the export market. During the mid-1970s, the United States withdrew from the Vietnam War and redirected its policy focus from Southeast Asia, thus greatly decreasing the amount of aid Thailand received. This change, combined with a decline in prices on the world market for agricultural goods, threatened Thailand's economic vitality.

During the 1970s and into the early 1980s, the decision-making agencies of the Thai government wavered and procrastinated on the question of changing to a focus on manufactured exports as a stimulus to sustaining economic growth. Entrenched economic interests pulled the government in the direction of continued support for agriculture and import substitution. But in 1984 a crisis brought on by economic recession resulting from government policies prompted a devaluation of the currency and the redirection of government services toward promotion of manufactured exports (Pasuk and Baker 1996b).

The government's indecision was caused, in part, by a dilemma between the Asian and Western models of economic growth. The Japanese model, followed by Korea and Taiwan, had two elements that had been absent from Thai economic policy. First, the government policy of these countries encouraged the development of very large conglomerate corporations. Government policy favored these large companies at the expense of the smaller by protecting the large firms from both domestic and foreign competition. In addition, these governments attempted to pick winners. Key industries were identified by the bureaucracy as crucial to industrial strength or with a high probability of being most competitive in the international market; these industries, then, were directed, supported, and protected by government action. In Thailand, on the other hand, government policy had not formally favored particular companies or industries, although it did so to some extent through corrupt practices (Pasuk and Baker 1998; Somsak 1993).

While Thai government policy flirted with these aspects of the Japanese development model until the mid-1980s, in the end Thailand rejected the emphasis on size and the practice of picking winners. As the economy began to grow rapidly after 1985, the pressure to implement these policies declined. Instead, Thailand embarked on a more liberal market-oriented economic policy. The previously limited financial market was opened to domestic and foreign investment, which encouraged the capital required by business, and most restrictions on competition that the large conglomerates had won in the preceding decades were eliminated. The government also pursued its traditional policy of macroeconomic stability. This means keeping the currency stable, inflation low, the government budget in balance, and the trade deficit to manageable proportions. The policies worked, and from 1985 to 1995 the Thai economy set out on a period of unprecedented growth, the highest rate of growth in the world.

Economic Crisis and the Future of the Thai Economy

By 1997, however, Thailand had hit another set of problems, but what in retrospect might be called only growing pains. The problem showed up most clearly in July 1997 when under pressure from international organizations and currency speculation the Thai government let its currency (the baht) "float." In other words, it allowed the baht to be traded like other currencies to find its own level of value in an open market rather than having it tied to the value of the U.S. dollar as in the past. Within a few months the baht had dropped from 25 to 1 U.S. dollar to 55 to 1 U.S. dollar.

Many of the details of the economic crisis beginning in 1997 need not concern us here. We can simply note Thailand had achieved the easy part of the industrialization process—labor-intensive export-oriented production—and would soon face competitive pressures (Akyuz 1998). Among the problems underlying the economic crisis were some overproduction and overcapacity in Asia generally, increasing competition from the poorer countries in the region with lower wages, and a newly liberalized financial system in Thailand that led to a lending boom of foreign funds into untenable and unproductive investments without proper governmental oversight (Jomo 1998). In short, the rich economic elites of Thailand were making deals to obtain loans of foreign money to get into the real estate bubble of the early 1990s based upon personal relations rather than sound economic principles, and government agencies that should have prevented this were looking the other way. The foreign funds expanded the bubble already inflated by domestic investment, creating what some have called "golf course capitalism" (Sesser 1993), in which far more resorts, expensive housing projects, and office buildings were built than could possibly be profitable, while neglecting the types of sustainable and productive economic investments that would offer employment and benefits to the rest of the people. When exports began to decline in 1996, foreign borrowing continued; but in 1997, the foreign exchange needed to pay back these loans was not available and a financial crisis ensued.

An immediate outcome of the economic crisis of 1997–98 was intervention by the International Monetary Fund (IMF) to loan Thailand money as the value of their currency dropped to a point where they could not repay loans coming due (Dixon 1999; Unger 1998). Such actions in developing countries around the world, along with similar interventions by the related World Bank, have been highly criticized in the past because of the power this gives the IMF and World Bank over these countries and because the political and economic changes dictated by these international organizations are often seen as helping the rich at the expense of the working class and poor in the developing countries (Bello, Cunningham, and Poh 1998).

While many Asian and American scholars view the IMF strategy in the Asian financial crisis as the wrong diagnosis of the wrong problem with the wrong remedies (Sachs 1997, 1998; Jomo 1998), at present it is too early to determine the outcome of the Asian economic crisis of the late 1990s and the situation of Thailand in particular. However, in the case of Thailand (and possibly some others in Southeast Asia) it may be suggested that intervention by the IMF is in a new situation. Thailand is now a nation with a relatively advanced economy, a relatively strong and responsible government bureaucracy, and greater economic affluence throughout the population (despite rapidly growing inequality in the 1990s that will be discussed in our chapter on social stratification). In essence, the IMF demands were focused on the financial system and led to the closing of inefficient and corrupt banks run by rich families that had helped fuel the bubble economy of the early 1990s. Thus, while it is too early to know for sure, it can be suggested that the IMF intervention has been more to the benefit of all Thais and their long-term economic future by forcing reform of a corrupt financial system that was more concerned with making the rich richer than with sound economic investments leading to jobs and steady growth benefiting all Thais.

CONCLUSION

While not typical in every respect, the Thai economy is much like those of other developing nations in East and Southeast Asia. After describing the basic nature of the Thai economy, we have shown how dependency in today's modern world system often prevents nations from achieving economic development and moving their people out of poverty. Thailand, however, has been moving rapidly in achieving this economic development, and despite the increasing income inequality of recent years, the standard of living for most Thais has improved, and poverty has dropped considerably.

We have devoted several pages to explaining how Thailand, along with some of the other developing countries in Asia, has done this because it is such an important topic. With the gap between the rich nations and poor nations expanding considerably in recent decades, and with world poverty growing steadily, we need a much better understanding of how economic growth can proceed to overcome the problems of the world's poor. Thailand, among some of the other nations of Asia, has shown that it can be done, and it is clear that the rest of the world could learn much from the record achieved by Thailand.

CHAPTER 4

The Thai Political System

A look around the world today clearly suggests that extensive economic development is associated with greater political democracy. This is to say, the educated population that is required by, and brought forth by, economic development does not mix well with dictatorship. Communist China, for example, is going through the process of conflict between old dictators and the most educated of their people—a conflict that came to a bloody head in 1989 when hundreds if not thousands of China's best educated were killed by the military in Tiananmen Square (Schell 1994). This process of conflict between old political elites and an increasingly educated population certainly varies from country to country. And we must be careful not to suggest that democracy will end up being the same in every fully developed country, nor is it to say that Western and Asian democratic systems will be the same. The process of democratization may take longer in one country, be more bloody in another, but conflict will occur in some form or another, until the country reaches more or less a steady state of high economic development and some degree and form of political democracy (Lenski 1966; Lenski, Lenski, and Nolan 1991).

Thailand is no exception. The Thais have even had a smaller version of China's Tiananmen Square massacre, with hundreds of students killed in the square of Thammasat University in Bangkok during extended protests over another military takeover of the government during 1976 (Kulick and Wilson 1996: 29; Keyes 1989: 993). The last round of such protests in 1992 was much less bloody ("only" some 50 to 100 deaths occurred), was more successful in that a military takeover was reversed, and led to much respect for the "cell phone mob" of middle-class professionals and office workers who took to the streets of Bangkok to support democracy (Pasuk and Baker 1996a; Murray 1996; Callahan 1998; Hata 1996).

Compared to the rest of Southeast Asia, Thailand's democratic achievements can be admired: While the Thai political system is certainly not a complete democracy today, when compared to Burma (or Myanmar as the new dictators demand the country be called), Cambodia, Laos, Vietnam, Indonesia, and even Malaysia, Thailand's political system is much more democratic, even though it is also quite chaotic, as we will see (Kulick and Wilson 1996: 177). In this chapter we will first consider some of the basics about the Thai political system, then turn to more details about its historical development and problems.

CHARACTERISTICS OF THE THAI POLITICAL SYSTEM

There are three aspects of the Thai political system that are most important to understand. First, like most relatively democratic nations of the world, and in contrast to the United States, Thailand has a parliamentary system of government. Second, again in contrast to the United States, like virtually all Asian nations (and most European nations in fact) Thailand has an unelected civil service or government bureaucracy that has extensive power in shaping and carrying out government policies. Third, like a few democratic nations such as England, Thailand has a constitutional monarchy; but the monarch is relatively unique, providing a powerful moral force in the nation, and has done so for more than 50 years. We can begin by approaching these subjects in turn.

Parliament

As with other nations that have adopted a **parliamentary system,** the Thai parliament has two houses. The lower house is the House of Representatives whose members (ministers of parliament, or MPs) are elected by a vote of the people. The country is divided into electoral constituencies on the basis of population (much like the House of Representatives in the United States), with one MP for every 150,000 people, and every constituency is guaranteed at least one member. Some of the constituencies have multimemberships with up to a maximum of three representatives. In all these cases election outcomes are determined by plurality, which means the candidate with the most votes wins even though it is not a majority. In the upper house, the Senate, members are appointed by the king with approval of the prime minister. It is in the Senate that military and bureaucratic authority is institutionalized, because by custom military officers down to the division commander level and bureaucrats at the rank of permanent undersecretary in the ministries are appointed along with many retired members from the same organizations. The Senate is the weaker body and cannot initiate legislation, but it can amend or block proposals passed by the House. Under a new constitution promulgated in 1998, in future elections senators will be elected and the lower house will comprise MPs elected from districts and others elected nationally from lists supplied by each party.

Changes in the characteristics of MPs over time give an indication of the development of the Thai political system. In 1969, for example, almost 60 percent of the members had less than a college education; in 1995, over 70 percent had undergraduate or advanced college degrees. The increasing prestige and importance of parliament and the increased legitimacy of political activity is indicated by the increase in the percentage of MPs identifying themselves as career politicians, from none in 1969 to over 50 percent in 1995 (King and LeGerfo 1996). Similarly, the occupational backgrounds of MPs have reflected the changes that have occurred in Thai society and the relative power of social groups. During the peak of military rule in the 1950s and 1960s, MPs with careers in the bureaucracy normally comprised between 20 to 25 percent of all members; after the September 1992 election they comprised only a little over 5 percent. While the proportion from business backgrounds was roughly equal to that of bureaucrats in the 1950s and 1960s, at least 50 percent of MPs came from business backgrounds after the 1992 election (computed from Pasuk and Baker 1996b: 338).

As is typical of a parliamentary system, the cabinet is the executive arm of the legislature. The head of the majority party or coalition of parties in parliament is the prime minister, and members of the prime minister's coalition are appointed to head the various cabinet ministries and serve as deputies both to the prime minister and within the cabinet departments. There are over 60 of these appointments in the Thai government.

Bureaucracy

The Thai parliament is still relatively weak compared to the permanent civil servants who run the ministries in the Thai government. The political system until recently was best characterized as a bureaucratic polity (Riggs 1966). Politics was primarily a conflict among various elements and factions within the military and bureaucracy, with very little public input. In fact, under the constitution, in many policy areas the Thai parliament can pass only general legislation and implementation is left to the government bureaucracy. An example might be a particular tax where the parliament can set the maximum rate but the bureaucracy manages the rate anywhere below that level. The bureaucrats also have much greater expertise than the elected officials, as well as extensive contacts within the government. Still, bureaucrats are not extremely powerful because elected politicians in the government can demote or transfer officials and can use this power to compel compliance. And as in parliament more generally, the official bosses of the bureaucrats, the prime minister's cabinet, reflects the change to greater control of government by business elites. As with elected governments most cabinet members have business backgrounds. Thus, the corporate elite influence government bureaucratic officials.

Despite all of this, however, on most details of government, the government bureaucrats have extensive power and independence, sometimes allowing them to take actions they believe are in the interests of the country as a whole rather than only the narrow interests of one group such as big business. The financial crisis that hit Thailand in 1997, though, has been attributed in part to the growing influence of business over the bureaucratic ministry officials, who otherwise would more likely have restrained the bubble economy of the early 1990s and required more sound lending policies by the big banks.

Monarchy

King Rama IX, Bhumibol Adulyadej, has reigned as constitutional monarch since 1946 following the mysterious and unsolved death of his brother, Anand, who was found shot to death in the palace. The monarchy's role was insignificant in politics after the end of its absolute status in the 1932 coup. But during the late 1950s, the military leader Marshall Sarit, with whom the king had established a friendship, reemphasized the symbolic role of the monarchy as a cornerstone of Thai identity and legitimacy for the government. Marshall Sarit also made the royal family extremely rich by returning the crown property that had been seized after the 1932 revolution.

Following this change in status, the king fostered the traditional conception of the king as "lord father," a semi-deity, a political and religious figure who is the embodiment of Thai culture. Rama IX, a jazz musician, inventor, and amateur sailor (who was born in Boston, Massachusetts, while his father attended Harvard University) took full advantage of the opportunity offered him. Not only did he perform the traditional rituals, he also made contact with the population, visiting every province, and initiated a large number of royally sponsored development projects in the countryside. Because of all this, and the simple force of his personality, the king is revered by almost all Thais, and it is this reverence that has created his political influence (Kulick and Wilson 1996; Terwiel 1991).

This is also to say that the king has *influence rather than power*. Despite the public esteem in which he is held, a determined military could depose him in a crisis situation. The monarchy is a useful institution in that it provides a focus for national unity and a prestigious and detached forum for mediation and compromise between political forces in times of conflict. In the eyes of a few people, however, the reliance of Thai society upon an institution from the past can be seen as a symptom of political underdevelopment, with the awe and deference awarded the king seen as maintaining traditional attitudes toward authority that to a large degree are incompatible with the political attitudes necessary for a modern democratic society. Despite all of this, though, the vast majority of Thais realize that for now the king remains the only umpire in the game of politics with the ability to influence and build links between the competing forces of society and the military during times of crisis.

DEMOCRATIC POLITICS THAI STYLE

Following daily events pertaining to Thai politics in a newspaper such as the *Bangkok Post*, one sees constant charges and countercharges of corruption, bickering and bargaining, and above all, it seems, indecisiveness in the face of severe problems confronting Thailand. At first, politics in Thailand appears to be complete chaos; it is very difficult to ascertain any patterns behind events or follow the dynamics of what seems part drama, part soap opera, and part tragedy. But despite appearances, there is an underlying structure and logic to Thai politics, as there is in most of the developing nations today that are rather new at the game of democratic politics. In what follows we will attempt to explain the forces at play that create the spectacle of Thai politics.

Elections

As the political system of Thailand has democratized, power has shifted away from the military and bureaucracy into the hands of those with money, and that means provincial businessmen (Robertson 1996). At the foundation of the electoral process are "vote-getting networks" headed by **jao-phor,** local "godfathers," the patrons at the head of localized patron-client networks in Thai politics. As we will see, much like the old city-ward politics of political "machines" in cities like Chicago in the United States, these local political networks serve many latent functions for community organization and welfare. As in the early U.S. ward politics, although these jao-phor, or godfathers, sometimes run for office in their own right, they often prefer to remain behind the scenes and exercise control through their ability to produce votes for candidates.

An example of how this system works is found in the northeastern town of Khon Khaen in the person of Sia Leng. From the 1950s to the present he has built a legitimate business empire and also developed illegitimate gambling businesses, one of which is an extremely popular underground lottery. The hundreds, perhaps thousands, of lottery sellers provide a ready-made network for vote-getting. When election time nears, the favors of money or forgiven debt to voters leads to their voting as Sia Leng directs them. Because of the extensiveness of the network, the permanent and stable contacts between lottery sellers and buyers, and Sia Leng's reputation, he can deliver enough votes in a number of constituencies to reliably deliver election victory to his chosen candidates (Somrudee 1993). Multimember constituencies that elect three MPs magnify the power inherent in control of such votes. Almost all rural provinces have this type of local power structure that can control the outcome of elections.

Networks may be based on legal or illegal businesses, control of important resources such as government funds and loans, or access to jobs in the legal business sector. As patrons, the godfathers also provide a range of services to their clients, such as food or transportation to the hospital in a time of need, which can be seen as important latent functions of these political machines in the face of weakly developed formal government offices to serve these needs. But of course these stable social networks are transformed into vote-getting networks at election time and can make jao-phor influential individuals in national politics. For instance, in 1987 a no-confidence motion against General Prem's government failed in part because the army chief of staff personally visited Sia Leng to solicit his assistance in persuading MPs under his control to withdraw support for the motion (Somrudee 1993; Ockey 1996).

At the next level up from the vote-getting networks is another set of patron-client networks in the form of *factions*. Factions can be divided into categories according to the strength of the ties that give them cohesiveness. The most cohesive factions are based on the ties of kinship, business connections, or vote-getting networks. In the case of these ties the costs of defecting from the faction are great and the basis for the ties difficult to replace. Factions based on vote-getting networks often have their source of cohesion outside of parliament in the person who controls votes in the MPs' constituencies, such as Sia Leng noted above, who does not meet legal criteria for entering parliament but is a force nonetheless.

Weaker cohesion is found in factions based upon ideological, regional, or personal factors. In these situations the cost of defecting from a faction is not great. Money-based factions constitute an intermediate grouping in terms of cohesiveness, while the most cohesive factions are those that have multiple ties and have all faction members in the same party. Factions often have members running in more than one party in order to increase the chance of obtaining a cabinet seat for the faction (Ockey 1996; Somrudee 1993.)

Political Parties

As in all democratic political systems, political parties in Thailand have been instituted to provide differing interest groups with a means of voice and representation in the political system. And as in all parliamentary political systems, in contrast to the U.S. political system, there are more of these political parties because voters often elect candidates from minor parties who at least have the chance to become power-brokers in a coalition government.

As is common, in Thailand these political parties are organized hierarchically, focus on particular personalities, and are comprised of, as described above, collections of patron-client networks, as well as one or more of the factions also described above. Wealthy businessmen, ex-generals, even gangsters become party leaders by offering campaign financing, the promise of cabinet positions, or direct financial payments as inducements to join. Party leaders are owed loyalty as long as the factions' and individual candidates' interests are advanced. Given the importance of factions and vote-getting networks, the parties remain regionally based, for example, with Democrats in the south, Chart Thai in the central region, and the New Aspiration Party in the northeast. Factions join parties on the basis of the probability of becoming a member of the governing coalition. Even in parliament, party leaders must sometimes make cash payments to their members to ensure their support during votes on important legislation.

Political parties in Thailand perform the usual democratic functions of fielding slates of candidates and contesting elections, but compared to parties in more established democracies they are not ideological or programmatic. During elections, appeals for votes are made on the basis of personality and potential or past benefits provided to the constituency. It must be emphasized that none of the political parties, with the possible exception of the Democrat party, Thailand's oldest, have an organized mass base with long-term allegiance (King and LeGerfo 1996).

Nongovernmental Organizations

Formally organized interest groups and nonprofit welfare organizations are often referred to as **nongovernmental organizations** (NGOs) in developing nations, including Thailand, to distinguish them from government-sponsored organizations designed to increase governmental control and implement policies that have been developed in government bureaucracies. As political development has progressed and politics liberalized, voluntary independent organizations (primarily NGOs) based on mutual concerns and performing a variety of social roles have proliferated. These organizations are now significant actors in the political arena, and in this section we focus exclusively on their political role.

Among organized political interests, big business is the only sector with well-established formal institutional links to the government. Among three levels of business organizations in Thailand, those at the apex are the big four—the Thailand Chamber of Commerce, the Board of Trade, the Federation of Thai Industries, and the Thai Bankers Association—all were created in the 1950s to represent the business elite. The function of these organizations is to consult with senior government officials, a process institutionalized in 1981 with the formation of the Joint Public-Private Consultative Committee (JPPCC). The JPPCC is comprised of representatives of the business organizations and senior bureaucrats and focuses on macro-economic policy making. It was through the JPPCC that the policy shift to export-led growth noted in the previous chapter was developed and adopted in the 1980s. Below this level are the less influential sectoral trade associations representing particular industries or firms, of which there are well over 200. At the third level, and least influential, are the provincial chambers of commerce linked as a network (Christensen 1993). Of all interest groups in the society, business groups, especially the largest corporations, are the most influential in affecting government policy.

Of increasing importance in the political arena is the growing array of NGOs that emerged and established themselves during the liberal period of the 1980s and now represent a wide variety of interests. There are organizations reflecting concerns regarding the environment and conservation, women, children, farmers, workers, education, AIDS victims, and prostitutes, to list only a few. Like the business interests and political parties, they are evidence of the more liberal political framework in Thailand that allows a greater scope of action for organized groups (Gohlert 1991; Sanitsuda 1994). At the social level they are vehicles providing an alternative to organization based on vertical patron-client relationships. They bring together individuals from a segment or segments of society on the basis of mutual interest, are not as hierarchical as traditional organizations, and provide an opportunity for issues to be addressed directly to the government.

The roles of NGOs in developing countries such as Thailand are not institutionalized like that of the business interests. There are no joint committees or regularized forms of communication for NGO participation in policy making. Thus, these NGOs must rely on the issuing reports, making public appeals, and taking direct action in the form of public protests and demonstrations to articulate their concerns and policy preferences to political decision makers.

The effectiveness of NGOs in policy making is limited, and successes are usually confined to specific projects. Even then their successes are often temporary. For instance, one large group, the Forum of the Poor, conducted extended demonstrations during 1997 and 1998, sometimes with as many as 10,000 demonstrators in Bangkok, and has developed an extensive program regarding farmers' economic, political, and social needs that it is seeking to have the government adopt. As an example of the how specific and limited NGO victories can be, one of the last acts of the outgoing Barnharn government in 1996 was the approval, bypassing a legally mandated environmental review, of the massive Kaeng Sua Ten dam project that had been shelved several years earlier after massive and prolonged protests organized by NGOs. Local villagers who would be displaced by the waters responded by putting death curses on the prime minister and four other cabinet ministers and threatened to harm anyone taking surveys for the dam project (*Bangkok Post*, November 25, 1996). As of this writing the curses have not worked, and of course the dam project is moving forward.

The Electorate(s)

When describing the electorate in Thailand we are really speaking of two electorates, the urban middle class and the poorer rural electorate. They differ in fundamental ways that contribute to the instability of Thai politics.

The middle class is comprised of salaried professionals, managers, technicians, scientists, educators, and small business owners. The existence of this class is a result of the rapid economic growth and industrialization of the last few decades. One observer notes that the core values of the new Thai middle class are pragmatism, materialism, and individualism (Girling 1996). Created by development, the new class depends on economic growth for continued prosperity, which in turn requires order and stability.

Polls taken during the 1996 election campaign reflect the urban middle class's concerns and modern orientation. In a Ramkamhaeng University poll almost 90 percent of the respondents were worried about the sluggish economy, with almost 55 percent saying that economic problems should have the highest priority for government. Only 31 percent thought political problems were most important (*Bangkok Post*, October 30, 1996). In another poll conducted by Suan Dusit Rajabhat Institute, over 38 percent ranked honesty as the most important qualification for a candidate to get their vote, followed by knowledge and ability (18 percent) and sincerity (17 percent) (*Bangkok Post*, September 30, 1996). The middle class desires efficient and honest government that promotes economic growth. It rejects military government because the economic incompetence, violence, and unpredictably such a government would provide does not meet these needs.

The middle-class orientation toward democracy is thus ambivalent. In an electoral contest the rural vote will dominate the small middle-class vote concentrated in Bangkok. Thai democracy does not deliver the honesty and efficiency desired and also directs government resources away from the urban sector and toward the provinces.

For the other Thailand, the rural population upon whom Thailand's economic development was built, a different set of orientations toward democracy and desires from government takes hold. Two factors are most salient regarding the rural sector. First, it has been controlled by government; and in the pursuit of Bangkok-based development, the rural sector has carried a disproportionate share of the burden. While Thai villages had a long history of self-governance with isolation and minimal interference from the central government, during the development era this has changed. Village headmen were absorbed into the lower levels of the Local Administration Department of the Interior Ministry, the Krom Karn Pok-Klong, the department for governing. These officials do rule, and rural people often refer to them as *nai*, a term used for the nobility under the monarchy (Akin 1996). Government control of the rural areas also increased under the threat of communist insurgency, extending the government's control and penetration of rural society.

The second factor affecting the rural population's orientation toward government is that it has remained traditional in its approach to politics. Old patterns of deference to those above one in the social hierarchy and reliance on the personal patron-client relationship have persisted. The government co-opted the rural populations' primary base for organized action, the village, while preventing its replacement with any other organizations not under the central government's control.

Economic development has led to an improvement in some basic conditions in the countryside, but over 90 percent of the households classified as poor are found in the rural population, and income and education remain low. The rural electorate has developed a direct material concern that political participation bring benefits to their villages and enhance their livelihoods, and elections are a means of making that happen. For a rural population governed by a remote Bangkok bureaucracy, patron-client relationships remain useful. If there is trouble with the police or arbitrary action by the bureaucracy, the villagers can look to a local patron for personal intervention on their behalf. If they elect a corrupt politician who is disliked by Bangkok voters, as long as that politician delivers roads, wells, dams, irrigation projects, schools, or other projects, then at least some visible resources are obtained. Politicians who succeed at this are thought to have *barami* (power), and if they are frequently seen by the constituency, provide some personal contact, and bring projects and protection, they are esteemed and respected by the rural electorate despite their flaws as perceived by urban people.

Given that both rural and urban voters are primarily just interested in specific benefits from politicians, general philosophical principles and party platforms are seldom stressed during elections. The candidates and parties primarily remind voters of what they have done in the past, promise generalities such as good government and representation, and emphasize the constituency specific benefits in the form of projects. One of the specific issues that concerns Bangkok voters, for example, is alleviation of traffic congestion. Given the centralization of government and the numerous agencies with administrative responsibilities for Bangkok, issues like traffic congestion have become the most hotly debated in recent elections.

THAI POLITICS TODAY: BASIC DEFICIENCIES

A combination of lack of expertise and severe competition for the limited resources of government has three major consequences for the state of Thai politics today. The first is instability. The competition for resources is very specific, focusing on individual contracts and benefits, and for the factions and parties in parliament it is a zero-sum game (Cristensen 1993). It may be useful to think of the resources available from the government as making up a big pie. If someone else has a piece, then by definition there is less for everyone else. So, if a particular faction wins in the game of extracting benefits and gains a contract or the granting of a license, all the other factions and parties are considered losers. The financial backers, vote-getting networks, and patron-client relationships that support a losing faction are then denied benefits; as a result, the parliament member's base of electoral support is threatened. This makes the stakes for the players very high in every case; thus, parties and factions have strong incentives to defect from the government coalition if they are denied rewards for membership. Defectors seek a better deal either immediately or as the outcome of a new election. The leader of the coalition stands upon a majority that is like a house of cards: At any moment the house may collapse under the strain of competition for benefits.

Associated with the instability is the second major consequence of the electoral system, a lack of policy coherence. General policies are very difficult to develop and implement, especially for the rural provinces, because such policies would mean a general or collective sharing of the government's resources. Policy making becomes very ad hoc, uncoordinated, and subject to obstruction and reversal, as parties and factions compete for particular advantage. If general policies were developed this would mean all provinces and constituencies would be treated equally, with no component of the electoral system getting any advantage over the others. At present such policies are almost impossible to adopt.

A recent and related effect of the domination of Thailand's political system by provincial politicians is the penetration of corruption into the macro decision-making agencies of government. Through the previous decades of economic and political development in Thailand, the macroeconomic policy-making agencies were somewhat removed from the worst of corrupt practices, especially the central bank and the Finance Ministry. The military and Bangkok-based business elites realized the importance of economic policy in achieving growth, and the agencies were left to the specialists and technocrats who had the expertise to manage economic affairs and provide financial stability. As provincial businessmen have gained ascendancy in parliament, however, these institutions have succumbed to the pressure of money politics.

This development has serious implications. Corruption in Thai politics has been known and accepted by foreign investors because it was peripheral to conducting successful business operations (see Kunio 1994). Not even the major Thai or international corporations can insulate themselves from corruption if it penetrates to these highest levels. In this regard Thailand stands to become like some other less developed countries where corruption is a serious impediment to economic growth.

CHAPTER 4

CONFLICT AND THE FUTURE OF THAI POLITICS:
A CONCLUSION

In Thai society there are two fundamental divisions that dominate politics. The first is the conflict between the military and the democratic elements in society. As the 1991 coup demonstrated, there are circumstances under which the military's domination is accepted, and there exist semidemocratic forces in the parties and factions that will accept military rule. The gradual movement of Thai society, however, is toward a more democratic system with greater constraints placed upon the military. If economic growth continues, the middle class becomes larger, and NGOs continue to proliferate and provide an alternative means of social and political organization, then the military will eventually be constrained to its professional role in providing security for the nation.

The second major conflict in Thai society demonstrates the importance of social development. This is the conflict that results from the uneven Bangkok-based development producing two societies, one living in the modern world and the other living in the past (Girling 1996). The urban middle class is actually ambivalent regarding democracy, and its commitment is conditional. Its individualist, materialist, pragmatic orientation fits with an honest, efficient, and technocratic democracy. Because only 10 percent of the seats in parliament are elected in Bangkok, when democracy is practiced, Bangkok loses. Rural society may remain in the traditional world of patron-client relationships and deference to authority, but in the practice of Thai democracy they do alter the emphasis on Bangkok. The corrupt politicians these rural people elect provide the projects and protection that a government chosen by only Bangkok voters would not provide. In their context, and with the alternatives offered them, the voting behavior of the rural electorate is no less rational than that of Bangkok voters (Anek 1996).

This conflict between rural and urban voters in Thailand today may be resolved in one of two ways. If time is allowed to take its course, and economic development continues its rapid pace, eventually the middle class will become large enough to dominate electoral politics; and if it wishes, it can pursue its own needs at the expense of the rest of society. The only other solution is for the middle class to come to grips with the needs of the rural sector and find a basis for common cause with them. For the foreseeable future, however, it is clear that Thailand will remain a semidemocratic country (Chai-Anan 1995), a country grappling with these conflicts.

CHAPTER 5

Social Stratification in Thailand

Americans who find themselves working closely with Thai people can make a real mess of things if they do not understand a few basic aspects of the Thai workplace. This is also to say that Americans must not bring to the Thai workplace typical American assumptions about how the boss and employees relate to each other.

Among Thai people, rank and authority are far more important than in the United States, and showing your respect to authority figures and following their demands without question is more likely deemed positive rather than negative as in the United States (Pye 1985: ix, 99). For example, an American manager in Thailand is unlikely to get much response if employees are invited to a meeting and asked to critique and suggest improvements to some aspect of company policy (Holmes and Suchada 1995). By doing so, Thais would feel they are indirectly criticizing superiors (something not usually done openly in the Thai society), and anyway, it is the job of their superiors to know such things.

Neither is the American manager likely to be successful in getting Thai employees to treat others openly and freely, without regard to rank within the company, level of education, or status of one's parents in the society. For Thais who have been so conditioned to respect hierarchy from the time they were small children, such behavior seems unnatural and difficult. An old saying in Thailand is *"roojak thee soong thee tam,"* which roughly means, "know who's high and low" (Holmes and Suchada 1995: 29).

Let's consider a very different kind of example related to the subject matter of this chapter. Looking across developing countries around the world, we find a clear pattern with respect to material inequalities: In country after country, the rich have been getting richer in recent decades, while conditions for most people have not improved, or even worsened. In Brazil, for example, the bottom 20 percent of the people receive around 2 percent of all the annual income, while the top 20 percent of people receive around 63 percent of all income (World Bank 1996: 237). As economic growth proceeds in these countries, it is typical that the rich own most of the companies benefiting from expansion, or the rich have strong ties to the outside multinational corporations that have come in to take advantage of the new development opportunities. For the masses, however, there is most often disruption in the countryside, with many pushed off their land or agricultural jobs and into the cities. In the cities, however, there are seldom enough jobs, and the jobs that do exist pay very poor wages. Multinational corporations from the rich countries are making their investments in the country precisely because wages are so low. Political leaders in these developing nations are not very interested in helping wages climb when they and their upper-class friends are getting rich because the multinational corporations are in the country. If wages increase, these multinationals are likely to leave (Chirot 1977: 122–45; Kerbo 1996: 425–27).

When we restrict our focus to the developing nations in East and Southeast Asia, however, we find a significantly different pattern: While inequality is high in a few of these nations, for the most part inequality is lower than in the developing countries of Latin America and Africa (Kerbo 1996: 417, 422). Thailand must be included among these Asian nations with lower income inequality, or at least until recently as we will see. With respect to poverty in Thailand, as development proceeded from the 1960s through the 1990s, by one standard measure, poverty has been reduced from about 50 percent of the population to 13 percent most recently. This is a remarkable feat when compared to other nations going through the process of economic development. As we will see in more detail in this chapter, when compared to most other nations in the world, advanced industrial nations or developing countries, Thailand presents us with an interesting contrast to many standard features of social stratification.

THE BASIC NATURE OF THAI SOCIAL STRATIFICATION

By **social stratification** we mean a system of ranking within the society, a system of ranking that has become well established and affects many things about how people live (Kerbo 1996: 11). There will always be some types of inequalities and a system of social stratification in all but the most simple societies. However, the level of these inequalities, and which are most important in affecting how people live, vary greatly around the world and through history.

As pointed out perhaps first by the French social scientist Alexis de Tocqueville in his famous book *Democracy in America* published in the 1830s, more than people from other Western nations, Americans lack a formal style of interaction and reject most rituals of status deference. There is equality in American social interaction. The assumption is, "I am just as good as anyone else," and there is an absence of the heavy status ranking such as found with the former dukes, duchesses, earls, and so forth of the old European world. The United States has the most unequal society among industrial nations of the late 1990s with respect to *wealth and income*, but when it comes to assumptions about a person's esteem, Americans are at least to some extent taught they are just as good as anyone else, no matter if they are poor. Ironically, despite the high levels of material inequality in the United States, nowhere else did the Western "enlightenment" and beliefs such as "equality and fraternity" and "equality of opportunity" catch on as much.

Such assumptions brought to Asia by the typical American can create what is called **culture shock,** a psychological condition sometimes created when confronting a culture quite different from one's own. Asian societies are steeped in hierarchy. For most Asians, and Thais in particular, it is hard to conceptualize a society in which all are ranked equally, or even remotely close to being equal. As noted by Louis Dumont (1970) in an insightful book *Homo Hierarchieus*, in most of Asia the Western ideal of equality is viewed as unnatural, unrealistic, and impossible (also see, Pye 1985: 99). As the noted Thai scholar John Girling describes it, Thais have an "authority culture" where "the assumption of superiority underlying the confidence of the ruling elite has its necessary counterpart in the *acceptance* of inferiority by those of lower status and those who lack organized power" (1981: 119).

To understand these rather non-Western values of ranking and social stratification, it is useful to begin by considering Max Weber's concepts of **class, status,** and **power** (or party). Weber offered a **multidimensional view of social stratification** in his criticism of Marx's one-dimensional view (Gerth and Mills 1946: 181–94; Kerbo 1996: 102–4). In addition to Marx's economic dimension of stratification, which stressed ownership versus nonownership of property as dividing people into different classes, Weber also described the importance of economic divisions based upon education and skill level. Then, Weber showed us how status ranking, or divisions based upon prestige and honor, along with divisions based upon power and authority in political and bureaucratic organizations in modern societies are also important, at times more important than economic stratification. Weber emphasized that all three dimensions of stratification (class, status, and power, or party) will exist in a society but that one or two of these dimensions will be more important, depending upon the kind of stratification system that exists in that society (Kerbo 1996: chap. 4).

As noted earlier in this book, the Asian emphasis on status ranking and authority is related to a collectivist value system in contrast to the Western individualist value system. Throughout most Asian societies, the greater importance of the group and the necessity of conforming to satisfy group needs are values shaped by centuries of wet rice agriculture; this value system and the acceptance of the rank order within it has resulted in Asian societies being generally different from those of Europe and North America.

There is, however, an additional aspect of the Thai belief system that makes status ranking even more important in Thailand than in many Asian nations. In his writings on the status dimension of social stratification, Weber used the example of the old Indian **caste system** as the **ideal type** stratification system based upon status. In this caste system, everyone's status ranking is determined at birth through an elaborate ranking of the person's family based upon the Hindu religion. One's rank is believed to be related to deeds in their past lives, and thus they have been reborn higher or lower in the caste system in this life because of these past deeds (Dumont 1970). The influence of the Hindu religion coming to Thailand from India combined with the Thai style of Buddhism resulted in the importance of *kamma* in Thailand, the belief that what happens in one's life is influenced by the accumulated store of deeds from previous lives. With this element of belief remaining strong in Thailand today it is quite understandable that a status dimension of social stratification remains strong (Akin 1996).

The Sakdina System

There is, however, more than just the influence of religion in Thailand's past that has led to an emphasis on status ranking and authority. In a rather remarkable and unique effort to clearly specify the exact rank order within the society, during Thailand's early kingdoms an elaborate stratification system known as **sakdina** was created (Akin 1996; Girling 1981: 25–26; Muscat 1994: 20–23). Often translated as "dignity marks system," the word *sakdi* is from Indian Sanskrit and means "power," and the Thai word *na* means "rice fields" (Keyes 1989: 29–30). In essence, then, the system of sakdina was developed to give everyone in the society an actual numerical ranking in terms of the number of people over whom they have authority, specifically authority over workers in the rice fields.

As can be seen in Table 5–1, the king's rank was so above all others he was not assigned a number. Just below, however, the second king was assigned 100,000 points, while the king's younger brothers and his sons held from 40,000 to 50,000 points. The point system then went lower and lower down the status ranks in the society to the bottom, represented in the 5 points given slaves. This table, however, only begins to outline the elaborate grading system that the sakdina system established and put into practice. Every individual in the kingdom received a ranking, and these rankings had practical implications. For example, in the legal system an infraction was deemed more severe if an individual committed

TABLE 5–1

Sakdina Rankings

Position in Society	Sakdina Score
Royalty	
King	Infinite
Upparat (second king)	100,000
Younger brothers or sons holding office	40,000–50,000
Younger brothers or sons without office	10,000–20,000
Younger brothers or sons (of concubines) in office	15,000
Younger brothers (of concubines) without office	7,000
Younger sons (of concubines) without office	6,000
Third-generation princes	1,500
Fourth-generation princes	500
Government officials	
Heads of household ministries	10,000
Heads of lesser ministries	5,000
Senior administrators	1,600–3,000
Middle-level administrators	400–1,400
Government employees	50–350
Buddhist monks	
Patriarchs versed in dhamma	2,400
Patriarchs not versed in dhamma	1,600
Monks versed in dhamma	600
Monks not versed in dhamma	400
Novices versed in dhamma	300
Novices not versed in dhamma	200
Commoners	
Skilled workmen and supervisors	25–30
Free peasants (*phrai luang* and *phrai som*)	10–25
Slaves	5

Sources: Akin 1996: 133–34; Reynolds 1987: 93.

an offense against someone of higher rank; if the relative rankings were reversed, the infraction was less severe (Wyatt 1984: 73).

This sakdina system of social stratification had its impact on Thai society even during the early days of the Chakri monarchy when the capital was moved to Bangkok; it was not officially eliminated until the military coup did away with absolute rule by the king in 1932. However, as you can imagine, a culture with many centuries of such a system as sakdina will likely require another century or more before its effects are significantly reduced, if they are ever reduced. And we can further understand why, as noted in beginning this chapter, equality remains such an unnatural concept for Thai people today.

INCOME INEQUALITIES IN THAILAND TODAY

As noted earlier in this chapter, when compared to other developing countries around the world, until recently, the level of income inequality in Thailand could not be considered high. Normally, high inequality exists within developing nations, while advanced industrial nations have lower levels. Simply put, as economic development moves a country to the stage of advanced nations today, the level of income inequality tends to drop with an increase in skilled occupations and a more educated labor force (Kerbo 1996: 416; Jackman 1975). This pattern of reduced inequality is not always consistent around the world, and in some early stages of economic development income inequality can fluctuate up and down to a large degree. But the general pattern of higher inequality among poorer nations can be seen in Table 5–2, which lists the percentages of income of the bottom 20 percent of people and the top 20 percent of people in various countries during the mid-1990s.

It is also worth noting that Thailand is not alone in having somewhat lower inequality for a developing nation: The same can be said for most other Asian developing nations around Thailand (listed at the top of Table 5–2) when compared to countries in Latin America and Africa. And we can also note that Thailand's level of income inequality was not much different from that of the United States, though we must recognize that the United States has the highest level of income inequality among advanced industrial nations (Kerbo 1996: 23).

One of the reasons for such lower inequality in Thailand compared to other developing nations has been the extensive land ownership among peasants throughout Thai history, which has kept these people from falling into very low income positions (Wyatt 1984: 9). But equally important, in contrast to the normal pattern for most other developing countries, especially in Latin America and Africa, as Thailand experienced rapid economic development from the 1960s through the 1980s the level of income inequality actually went down instead of up. Even more dramatic was the drop in the poverty rate. During the 1950s the level of poverty was around 50 percent in Thailand, dropping to 23 percent by the early 1980s (Pasuk and Baker 1998: 282).

But during Thailand's rapid economic development and bubble economy of the late 1980s and 1990s, until it all came to a crashing stop in 1997, the pattern of relatively low inequality for a developing country changed dramatically. As we have noted in earlier chapters, it was an economic boom for the rich more than anyone else. Millions were being made by real estate developers with what was now called "golf course capitalism." Bankers were getting wealthy loaning money for it all, and

TABLE 5–2

Comparison of Income Inequality within Developing Nations

Country	Percentage of Total Household Income	
	Poorest 20%	Top 20%
Thailand	5.0%	52.7%
Bangladesh	9.4	37.9
Indonesia	8.4	43.1
Philippines	5.9	49.6
Malaysia	4.6	53.7
Vietnam	7.8	44.0
El Salvador	3.7	54.4
Egypt	8.7	41.1
Peru	4.9	50.4
Chile	3.5	60.1
Costa Rica	4.0	51.8
Brazil	2.5	64.2
Panama	2.0	60.1
Mexico	4.1	65.3
Venezuela	4.3	51.8
Kenya	3.4	62.1
Zambia	3.9	50.4

Source: Table constructed from data presented in *World Development Report* (World Bank 1999: 198–99). Data are from years during the mid-1990s.

the well-educated people in Bangkok were bringing in huge incomes with the big labor shortage created by the overheated economic expansion.

As a consequence, the average income of the top 10 percent of the people tripled during this time period, while the average income of the bottom 30 percent of the people, and most of the other 60 percent, was little changed (Pasuk and Baker 1998: 285). Likewise, while urban people had incomes of 2.5 times that of rural people in the early 1980s, the gap was over 4.0 by the early 1990s.

The decline in poverty, however, continued. While the rich were getting richer during the boom years of the late 1980s and early 1990s, at least the poor were not getting poorer. In fact, recent government figures on poverty in Thailand show that poverty dropped to just over 11 percent of the population by 1996 (*Bangkok Post*, April 21, 1998). These government data on poverty seem to use a very limited definition of the poverty line (what it costs to buy basic necessities), but even though a "true" poverty rate may be higher, the point is that however it was measured it did not get worse.

With unemployment rising rapidly during 1997 and 1998 with the economic crisis resulting from the burst bubble economy, however, no one yet knows the extent to which poverty has gone back up. It has not likely gone up as much as one would expect, though, because many of those made redundant (losing jobs) were recent immigrants to the urban areas and they have simply returned to their farms where production is still sufficient. Incomes of the rich, on the other hand, have dropped dramatically, likely reversing in short order the growth of inequality during the late 1980s and early 1990s. For example, while a few Thai families were listed among the world's billionaires in *Forbes* magazine during the early 1990s, by 1997 there were none.

Rural-Urban Inequalities

Before leaving the topic of general inequalities in Thailand, it is important to consider the level of inequality between people living in major cities (especially Bangkok and Chiang Mai) and the countryside. This is an important topic in almost all developing societies because of the typical pattern of *uneven development*—some sectors of the economy develop more quickly than do others, and some not at all. And when a developing country becomes tied to the world market for agriculture, as usually happens in the process of economic development, agricultural areas are severely disrupted (Kerbo 1996: 415–16; Chirot 1986). Before rapid economic development and becoming tied to the world market for agriculture, it did not make economic sense in traditional agricultural areas to use all the land or move to capital-intensive agriculture (employing fewer peasants but more machines) because there was no real market for new production. When brought into the world agricultural market, all of this changes. There are "land enclosures," meaning more land is taken away from the small land-owning peasants by rich land owners, and more machines and chemicals begin putting peasants out of work. Wealthy land owners usually become even richer when the agricultural area turns to the world market for exports, but peasants lose their land, their jobs, and even food, which is then being shipped out of the country. Most often these peasants are pushed into the big cities in desperate searches for work. As a consequence, of course, inequality between the rural and urban areas grows rapidly. Aid projects involving what was called the **green revolution** were started many years ago by international agencies and usually made the situation worse. More agricultural technology was introduced, improving agricultural output significantly; and even more peasants were put out of work, widening the gap between the rich and poor.

The above description of agricultural disruption and growing rural-urban inequality has been happening in Thailand, but only to some extent when compared to most developing nations. It is important to know that in contrast to most developing countries today, Thai peasants have always been much more likely to own their own land. Also, because of the old tradition discussed earlier that in theory the king owned all land in Thailand and his subjects were given the privilege of using this land, there was not a system of large estates held by wealthy landlords (Kulick and Wilson 1996: 132; Pasuk and Baker 1996a: 143; 1996b: 396). Finally, it is important to remember that overpopulation has never been a problem in Thailand's rural past; in fact, it was usually the opposite. A result has been plenty of land for peasants ready to work their own plots. Thai peasants, consequently, have always been rather proud and independent, with relatively little inequality in the countryside compared to most other developing countries around the world.

The figures on inequality noted above do show that since the 1950s there has been growing rural-urban inequality (a rural-urban gap of 2.5 to one growing to 4.0 to one). Government policies had been favoring low agricultural prices for urban workers as a means to further the new development policies directed toward industrial growth. Still, with a new awareness of the growing inequality, the Thai government and the king have created and expanded rural development projects. Poverty continues to go down in the rural areas, but less than in the urban areas. For example, the new poverty data released by the Thai government in 1998 show the primarily rural areas (such as northeastern Thailand) have a poverty rate of 19 percent compared to 11 percent for the country over all (*Bangkok Post*, April 12, 1998). But, as noted above, there are 4 million rural people temporarily living in Bangkok who are losing their jobs, and many will be moving back to the rural areas. This will no doubt further increase the poverty rate in rural areas. As a result, new protest groups are active to promote new government policies favoring the rural poor (Gohlert 1991). The new social movement group Forum for the Poor, for example, staged massive protests in Bangkok during 1998 and will likely continue such protests.

THE UPPER CLASS, CORPORATE CLASS, AND WEALTHY

Even though their wealth has been somewhat diminished by the economic crash of 1997, there is certainly still a wealthy class in Thailand today. In precise terms, an **upper class** is made up of people who are in the highest status order within a society as well as being wealthy (Kerbo 1996: 159; Baltzell 1958; Domhoff 1998). In old feudal societies this group is most simple to locate; they are the titled aristocrats such as dukes, duchesses, earls, and so forth found all over the world. In reality, of course, in addition to being a status elite, these people tend to have most of the wealth and thus dominate the economy as well. As the advanced industrial societies developed, though, the overlap between upper-class status ranking and wealth, especially corporate wealth, has become more complex. A somewhat separate class that we can call a **corporate class** has emerged; these people often lack upper-class status, but they are able to own or control the biggest corporations in the society.

In many Southeast Asian nations (Thailand, Malaysia, and Indonesia especially) we also find this complexity between an upper class and corporate class, but for different reasons. With old traditions of royalty there is clearly an upper-class status in these nations. In Thailand, as we have seen, a long history of royalty with kings having many children has resulted in a large upper class of people with various claims to royal ancestry. This titled upper class in Thailand has extensive advantage in obtaining high professional and corporate positions, but they are often not among the most wealthy in the society.

The current king of Thailand is very wealthy, owning a large percentage of Thai real estate and corporate stock. As we have seen, in old Thailand the king in theory owned everything, especially the land, and peasants were allowed to live on and work the land under the grace of the king. With the 1932 coup deposing of the all-powerful monarchy in Thailand, much of the king's wealth was taken as well. After the current Thai king ascended to the thrown in the late 1940s, however, much of the crown property was returned. All over Thailand today you can find offices of the Crown Properties Bureau that manages the king's wealth and property. King Bhumibol even has a controlling interest in one of the largest banks in Thailand, Siam Commercial Bank, and the biggest conglomerate, Siam Cement Co. But unlike the typical rich monarch, King Bhumibol lives modestly and uses most of his time, and much of his wealth, promoting social welfare projects throughout Thailand (Kulick and Wilson 1996: 53–57). Though in his 70s, the king can still be seen all over Thailand promoting various new agricultural projects for poor peasants, displaced hill tribe people, and the poor of all backgrounds in Thailand.

With the exception of the king, the group with economic power in Thailand today best fits the classification of a corporate class. Much like Japan before World War II with its *zaibatsu* and much like South Korea today with its *chaebol* (Kerbo and McKinstry 1995; Kim 1997), Thailand today has a corporate class of wealthy families that own and control most of the country's biggest corporations. For example, there are four main family groups that control much of the economy through their control of large banks and corporate conglomerates, as listed below (Muscat 1994: 115):

Bangkok Bank—Sophonpanich family

Thai Farmers Bank—Lamsam family

Bangkok Metropolitan Bank—Tejapaibul family

Bank of Ayudhya and Siam City Bank—Ratanarak family

Before the 1997 economic crisis started a process of shifting corporate ownership among the biggest financial institutions, which is still in progress, seven of the top 16 banks in Thailand were controlled by one of these four families (Muscat 1994: 117).

The biggest corporate conglomerate of them all, however, is the Charoen Pokphand Company, or simply the CP Group as they are popularly known in Thailand. By 1995 the CP Group had 300 large companies, with 80,000 employees and branches in 20 countries. The CP Group supplies most of Thailand's chickens, eggs, and pigs, among other big agribusinesses; they are a major player in the new high-tech telecommunications industry in Thailand and have moved into retailing with control of the Thai franchises of 7-Eleven, KFC, Wal-Mart, Makro, and others all over Thailand. In China they now make motorcycles, distribute petroleum, make beer, and help develop real estate (Pasuk and Baker 1998: 11).

The history of Thailand and other Southeast Asian countries, however, has resulted in a rather unique corporate class: The vast majority of the most wealthy corporate families are people of Chinese ancestry. All but two of the richest 25 businessmen in Thailand today are of Chinese heritage, and two of the largest three corporate conglomerates, including the CP Group, are dominated by Chinese business families (Kulick and Wilson 1996: 90). Further, 12 of the top 15 banks are controlled by families of Chinese heritage (*International Herald Tribune,* April 17, 1998). As we will see later, what is even more remarkable for Thailand is that in the face of all the economic dominance by people of Chinese heritage, there has been comparatively little resentment of the Chinese-Thais, and almost no violence against them. This is in striking contrast to neighboring Indonesia and Malaysia where people of Chinese heritage also dominate the economy; in Indonesia, thousands of these Chinese have been killed in rioting against them over the years, and many hundreds in Malaysia as well (Kulick and Wilson 1996: 85).

The Corporate Class and the Thai Military

We should not leave the subject of corporate elites without mention of the position of the Thai military. In what always sounds odd to people of the advanced industrial nations of North America and Europe, throughout the developing countries of Asia there is often direct military involvement in the economy. It is not simply that the military influences the political system and thus private corporations through control over the government. This of course happens when military coups take control of governments, not so uncommon in the history of developing countries all over the world. Rather, in a few Asian countries such as China and Thailand, the military *owns* or has major stock control of banks, media firms, and factories of various kinds. Further, top generals are often brought into the boards of directors of many corporations where the military has no major stock ownership (Pasuk and Baker 1998: 22).

Since the military coup of 1932 that put an end to the absolute monarchy in Thailand, one avenue for getting rich, in fact, has been through the military. As negative as this may sound to people of Western societies, and despite the extensive corruption such military economic activity creates, there are actually some positive aspects of the military-corporate alliance for Thailand. First, with the extensive dominance of the economy by ethnic Chinese in Thailand, the military-corporate alliance has helped reduce anger directed toward the ethnic Chinese (Muscat 1994: 57, 83). In direct contrast to what has happened in neighboring Indonesia and Malaysia in recent decades, the Thai military is unlikely to allow violent attacks on the rich ethnic Chinese in Thailand. Second, with few opportunities for professional and economic mobility for poor peasant boys, the Thai military provides one of the few institutions with some equality of opportunity. A peasant boy does have some hope of following a version of the American "log cabin" story: He can join the military, move up the ranks, become a general, find himself on the boards of big corporations, retire to a top managerial position in a corporation, or, as is not uncommon, marry the daughter of a senior general along the way to inherit some of that family wealth (Wyatt 1984: 273). In other words, this is a case of what sociologists often call *functional alternatives* to needed benefits in a society (Merton 1957). In this case it is a functional alternative to more equality of opportunity in the Thai economy.

THAI LABOR: STRUGGLES IN A DEVELOPING ECONOMY

Developing countries are not generally known as places allowing for much political or economic democracy. The latter usually refers to the ability of workers, through labor unions, to influence what happens to them in the workplace and to influence political policies to help the working class. Extensive cross-national research has shown that almost all developing countries have weak or nonexistent labor unions (Bornschier and Ballmer-Cao 1979). Thailand is no exception. Also typical, Thai workers have not been passive; but they have struggled in attempts to establish labor unions and take political action.

With economic development slowly moving ahead in the 1940s, Thai labor unions first became active (Pasuk and Baker 1996a: 100–6). But military government activity to suppress labor unions by the late 1940s led to violent strikes and ultimately to the destruction of labor-union strength. With a military government temporarily out of power between 1973 and 1976, unions became more active; but they again faced violent repression by 1976. Finally, with civilian governments in Thailand since the early 1990s, there is some increase in union membership and activity, however slow and weak. There are now two labor federations, LCT and

TTUC, with some 300,000 members. The Thai government has recently enacted a few laws attempting to protect working conditions and wages for labor (*Bangkok Post,* February 27, 1997), but it remains to be seen how effective these laws will be.

Thus, while wages and working conditions for Thai workers have improved, Thai workers have a very long way to go in catching up to workers in developed nations (Levine 1997). Work in Thailand is still dangerous despite laws designed to make the workplaces safer, either because such laws are ignored, due to too few inspectors, or because of bribes to inspectors. Minimum wage laws are also often ignored, labor unions are still commonly refused access to factories, and often workers who join unions are fired. Our personal interviews with Thai, Japanese, and American managers of several large corporations, along with 1,000 questionnaires received from workers, confirm that many of the corporations have managed to avoid unionized workers—we must note, however, that the American corporations in Thailand have been more accepting of unions and more often had unionized workers. Japanese managers in particular spoke to us of their fear of unions (Kerbo and Slagter 1996). One technique that has reduced union activity for most multinational firms in Thailand is a heavy reliance of short-term labor by young females; approximately 80 percent of workers in these export-oriented firms are female (Pasuk and Baker 1996a: 98).

GENDER INEQUALITIES

The image of **gender** relations and inequalities in Asia is primarily negative in the eyes of people from Western nations. Many details of the place of women in Thailand, past and present, do not help this image. Guides taking you through the beautiful Grand Palace (the residence of the kings during the Bangkok period until recent decades) and the attached *Wat Phra Kaew* are unlikely to tell you that one compound housed a "city of women" (a harem) with approximately 3,000 women at the service of the king (Shearer 1989: 56–58). In the past, male members of the extended royal family had multiple wives, and kings sometimes had 50 or more children with several wives. As for other negative images, currently there are estimates of some 800,000 prostitutes working in Thailand, more than the number of Buddhist monks or school teachers.

While there is plenty of evidence in support of the usual image of women with low status in Thailand, there is also evidence which runs counter to this image. Put another way, there is a confusing complexity in the position of women in Thailand today. On the one hand, the opportunities for Thai women in the economy and professions are comparatively good (Kulick and Wilson 1996: 77–79; Pasuk and Baker 1996a: 111–14). For example, compared to advanced industrial nations of

Europe and North America, a high percentage of Thai corporate executives and board members are women. Of the top 10 exporting corporations accounting for much of Thailand's rapid growth in the 1980s and early 1990s, 7 had a majority of women at the top. In medicine, universities, and other professions, women account for a large percentage of the positions. Overall, female participation in the labor force is 70 percent, among the highest in the world. And in a particularly striking contrast when compared to statistics of other developing countries, and those all over Asia, women account for approximately 50 percent of university students in Thailand.

On the other hand, in elected positions and within the government ministries, and certainly the military, women are extensively under-represented (Pasuk and Baker 1996a: 111–14), though Thai women were the first able to vote in Asia (Kulick and Wilson 1996: 72). And, of course, there is the massive problem of prostitution, involving children and sex slaves (discussed more fully in a later chapter), which seems to be completely at odds with the positive positions of women in the Thai society.

As always, when we want to understand a subject such as the position of women in Thailand today, we must begin with past traditions and how they were formed to see how they have shaped the present. When doing so we find there have been a number of cross-currents affecting Thai women, though social scientists agree one traditional practice has favored the status of Thai women: a **matrilocal,** if not a **matrilineal,** family system in most of Thailand's peasant areas. A matrilocal family system refers to one in which the female inherits the land while the man she marries moves onto her land and that of her family. A matrilineal family system simply means the female line of ancestors is more recognized as the most important family line, in contrast to the **patrilineal** family system most common around the world.

The best description of rural Thailand's family system over the centuries would be **unilineal** in that no family names were present at all. One of the kings of Thailand recognized less than 100 years ago that in dealings with the West family names would be useful, so he ordered Thais to have one (Wyatt 1984: 5). Thus, even though the family line of either side of the marriage was less important, the female usually inherited the land, requiring her husband to come and work this land to prove himself to his new relatives. It is not difficult to see that this tradition gave women a distinct advantage with respect to influence in the family (Girling 1981: 5).

If this matrilocal system was dominant all over Thailand, of course, we could expect the position of women to be even stronger than it is today; but such was not the case. There is still disagreement among anthropologists over how widespread this matrilocal system was in Thailand, but it is clear there was a mix: The matrilocal system was predominant in northern Thailand, while a patrilineal and partilocal system was predominant in the south, especially as one moved further down to the Islamic-dominated areas of Thailand today.

There is, however, even more complexity in Thailand's family traditions. More than 100 years ago many Chinese began moving into Thailand, bringing their patrilineal traditions. As we will see in more detail below, there has been extensive assimilation of the ethnic Chinese into the Thai mainstream, and the same goes for many of their traditions.

Further, adding another layer of complexity, there was always a big split between the urban nobility and peasant traditions in Thailand. Unlike rural people, the urban-based nobility were patrilineal to the extreme, with women very subservient to their fathers and then to their husbands. And in rural areas there was no strong tradition of arranged marriages, while such were common among the urban nobility of Thailand (Girling 1981: 41).

Overall, at least we can conclude that when compared to other women of East Asia and Southeast Asia, such as China, Korea, and Japan, the position of Thai women is higher. And this is especially so within the economy, professions, and the home, if not in politics.

RACE AND ETHNIC INEQUALITIES

One of the most persistent and growing problems in the world today is racial and ethnic conflict. In recent years there have been many cases of mass killings, or more precisely, **genocide** aimed at "ethnic cleansing," as seen in the former Yugoslavia and several countries in Africa. Closer to Thailand, we have already noted that in the second half of the 20th century alone there have been mass killings of ethnic Chinese in Indonesia, with estimates of hundreds of thousands killed (Kulick and Wilson 1996). In the face of all this, Thai people can be quite proud of the past and present relations between racial and ethnic groups in their country.

And there are many such groups in the country: ethnic Chinese, Muslims in southern Thailand, ethnic Laos, Cambodians, Burmese, Indians who moved around Asia with the expansion of the British Empire, and of course **hill tribes.** The hill tribe people have lived all over Southeast Asia, giving little respect to national borders and found mostly in the northern regions of Thailand. These hill tribes with their colorful clothing and traditions include Karen, Mon, Akha, Lisu, and Lahu along with other smaller groups. Chinese make up the biggest ethnic group in Thailand, though there has been so much assimilation that the definition of who is Chinese is difficult, and the best estimate is perhaps 10 percent of the population over all, with a much larger percentage in Bangkok. Ethnic Muslims also make up about 10 percent of the Thai population, but they account for about 80 percent of the population in the four most southern provinces of Thailand.

Hill tribe—Hill tribe children of northern Thailand, many of whom are dressed in their traditional style of colorful hand woven clothing.

There have been some prejudice and discrimination against the Islamic Thais and, because they are often so poor, the ethnic Laos from the northeast of Thailand. And there have been old conflicts between the "low-lander" Thai people and the "high-lander" hill tribe people over land use and ownership. But the greatest potential for ethnic conflict, as with Thailand's neighbors, was with the ethnic Chinese because of their dominance of the economy. During the 1920s there were some attacks on the ethnic Chinese by the quasi-fascist "Wild Tigers" paramilitary group (Kulick and Wilson 1996: 85), but there have been no systematic attacks on ethnic Chinese or other racial or ethnic groups since.

It is suggested that the Thai style of Buddhism, with its acceptance of many peoples, has not predisposed Thais to much ethnic hatred. And we have already seen how the new military rulers of Thailand took up the chance to cooperate economically with these ethnic Chinese for the interests of both. In addition, in the 1950s the Thai government, realizing the potential for conflicts, started educational programs in the schools to overcome ethnic prejudice. A result of all this has been a rather easy assimilation of ethnic Chinese so that in big cities it is sometimes difficult to find a Thai person who does not claim at least some distant Chinese heritage (Pasuk and Baker 1998: 13–17).

The most significant ethnic conflict found in Thailand has been between the southern Muslims and the Thai government. Earlier in this century, and long before, the people of the four southern provinces of Thailand were a part of Malaysia, a country that is 90 percent Muslim. Thus, when these people found themselves to be a part of Thailand, they suspected discrimination and prejudice, which certainly had some basis in fact. These southern Islamic provinces have historically not received the same economic development and government attention as the rest of the country, and they remain poorer today.

With some political violence by the Pattani United Liberation Organization and similar organizations in recent decades, there has been more government attention to the plight of these southern Thais. There have been many new economic development projects, some directed by the king himself. As the 20th century ends it seems such efforts have been successful, with the Islamic separatists almost extinguished and better prospects for economic development in this region (see various issues of the *Bangkok Post,* January 1998).

CONCLUSION

With respect to social stratification in general, the two most prominent features of Thailand are status ranking and, until recently, comparatively low levels of material inequalities. The old traditions of status and authority ranking in the Thai culture will no doubt continue to have their impact. In his famous survey of people in 50 nations, Hofstede (1991: 26) included one scale, the "power-distance index," that best taps the type of status and authority ranking we have described for Thailand. Among these 50 nations, Thailand had one of the highest scores on "power-distance" in the culture.

With respect to material inequalities, on the other hand, Thailand is now going through a period of change and disruption. The economic crisis that hit most of Southeast Asia in 1997, and Thailand first, will be played out over the next several years. The bubble economy of the late 1980s and early 1990s that preceded and helped cause the economic crisis of 1997 quickly overturned Thailand's position of relative equality among developing nations. The rich got richer, and quickly, on stock and real estate speculation with so much economic expansion focused on projects favoring the rich. When this came crashing down in 1997, the rich lost millions, but the rest of the people also lost jobs. In just over a year some 2 million additional unemployed appeared in Thailand.

How Thailand moves out of economic crisis in 1999 and beyond will have a big impact on the future of inequality and social stratification in the country. It is at the crossroads, so to speak. With intelligent policies Thailand can reestablish a more gradual and broad style of economic development that will raise the standards of living of all Thais, as had been more the case with Thai economic development earlier. For now, however, the direction of economic policies is in the stage of political debate, and the future is still to be determined.

CHAPTER 6

Religion in Thailand

One of the quickest ways to see the real Bangkok, that is, the Bangkok where most Thais live and work, is to take a boat through the many *klongs* (canals) of the city. Moving through any of these klongs, one sees the houses of the working class and middle class (the rich live further out of the city in most cases), beautiful tropical plants (which provide a contrast to the polluted water in which they are growing), children playing (often swimming in the polluted water), and women going to floating markets (or the markets coming to them in little boats). Perhaps more than anything else, however, Westerners are struck by the many beautiful **wats** (Buddhist temples or small churches) in every neighborhood all over Bangkok and in every provincial city or rural village. With their steep tile roofs of orange, green, and red, and the strange looking demons and gods guarding the steps, these wats certainly look different from the community churches of Western cities in Europe and North America. But their functions are remarkably similar.

Local people come to these neighborhood wats for prayer, community worship, funerals, and important religious holidays, as well as for local carnivals and important town meetings. And the men inside who are in charge of the wats, the Buddhist monks who give the religious teachings, are neighborhood saints with a similar mix of characteristics as the local religious leaders in Europe and North America: They do their jobs with strong faith and diligence but sometimes succumb to human frailties.

Among countries that have achieved at least some form of advanced agrarian economic development, in most respects religion looks rather similar all over the world. There are important beliefs about what is right and wrong and where people came from and where they are going; and there are community centers where people come in search of moral guidance and affirmation and to take part in religious ceremonies, many associated with the most significant life events—birth, marriage, and death. Thailand is no different.

In this chapter our subject is the basic institution of religion in Thailand. We will find that while those Buddhist monks in orange robes found all over the country look exotic to Western eyes and that the Buddhist philosophy seems completely different from Western religion, there are aspects of the function and role of religion that are similar and more familiar to the Westerner than one would first imagine.

RELIGION IN THAILAND: AN INTRODUCTION

Over 90 percent of the people of Thailand practice **Buddhism,** with **Islam** accounting for most of the remaining 10 percent of the population. In the four southern provinces of Thailand on the Malay peninsula, with a substantial proportion of indigenous Malays, Islam is predominant. But there is also a significant population of Muslims in Bangkok who are highly integrated into the social fabric of the city, even though there are distinct Muslim neighborhoods centered around mosques that can be found scattered among the much more numerous Buddhist temples. In far southern Thailand, on the other hand, the majority of Muslims are less integrated into the mainstream of Thai society and retain a cultural as well as religious distinctiveness. And there are some Christians. But despite centuries of a Christian presence in Thailand, the Christian religion has made few inroads against the predominant Buddhist religion.

Buddha—A typical Buddha image in a temple. In the foreground are many candles presented as merit-making gifts or in response to the fulfillment of requests people made at the temple.

It is also important to know that not only do 90 percent of the Thai people claim to be Buddhist, they are for the most part serious about their religion, as are the other approximately 10 percent of the Thai population who are Muslim. This is in contrast, for example, to modern Japan where most people do not find religion to be very important in their lives, although they continue to follow the old Buddhist and native Japanese Shinto religious rituals during life's special occasions, such as at weddings, funerals, births, and important holidays such as New Year (Kerbo and McKinstry 1998). As we will see, Thai people normally feel their religion strongly, and it has a major impact on their lives and thinking.

The pervasiveness of religious beliefs in Thailand is demonstrated by the data in Table 6–1. Large percentages across all sectors of the Thai populations believe in most of the basic aspects of Buddhism, as well as other spirit beliefs to be described in detail below. From a sociological perspective, the data in Table 6–1 also confirm findings regarding religion generally in almost all societies. Women appear to be somewhat more religious than men, and older, less educated, and rural people are more religious than the younger, more educated, and urban people with regard to Buddhist beliefs. But with regard to the more animist or "superstitious" beliefs, there are some interesting anomalies apparent in Thai society. For example, younger Thais are more likely to make vows to spirits; the more educated are more likely to engage in spiritualism and fortune-telling; and urban people are significantly more likely to practice both types. This suggests that economic development has had a slightly greater impact in diminishing the significance of Buddhism than it has the animistic-spiritualistic elements of Thai religion.

A remarkable indicator of the Thai respect for religion is the fact that some 80 to 90 percent of *all* young males who identify with Buddhism in Thailand become monks for at least a few months in their lives—usually in their late teens or early 20s. While monks, they live the usual spartan life in their monasteries, sleeping on the floor, abstaining from all drugs, alcohol, and sexual activity, abstaining from eating after midday, all the while meditating and learning Buddha's teachings. So accepted is the tradition of all young men entering the monastery at least briefly that private corporations and government agencies must give automatic time off from work for them to do so. Traveling around Thailand, but especially in the month of August during Buddhist Lent, one will often find a procession of people, usually following a small pick-up truck. In the truck is the honored young man, head shaven and dressed in white, on his way to the monastery, with dozens of family and friends following behind to see him off. The night before this procession the whole village is likely to have had a big party in honor of the young man, with his parents paying large sums of money to provide food, drink, and entertainment for the whole village.

TABLE 6-1

The Distribution of Religious Beliefs and Practices
in the Thai Population

| Category | Buddhist Related Beliefs | | Animistic-Spiritualistic Beliefs | |
	People Have Unequal Good Kamma	Bad Kamma Causes Negative Consequence	Fortune-Telling, Palmistry, Astrology	Making a Vow to Spirits
All	65.20%	75.10%	39.20%	38.80%
Male	62.80	71.60	32.10	32.10
Female	71.50	81.00	50.10	50.20
Age				
15–19	56.60	67.50	37.90	56.20
20–29	55.80	65.40	37.70	38.30
30–39	75.70	81.10	38.30	37.80
40–49	79.00	86.60	38.70	34.40
50–59	82.00	95.90	43.60	32.50
60 & over	83.30	96.70	31.00	17.20
Education				
0–4 years	91.50	95.60	29.90	31.90
7 years	86.60	89.00	38.10	35.40
10 years	82.80	89.10	40.40	34.50
12 years	81.30	78.10	40.40	45.10
Vocational	82.50	84.70	42.70	43.50
Bachelors	64.30	78.20	45.10	36.50
Graduate	61.50	67.00	47.00	34.90
Urban-rural				
Bangkok	59.60	69.50	41.10	40.40
Rural	76.40	83.80	34.10	35.50

Source: Table constructed from data presented by Suntaree (1991: 172–85).

BUDDHISM

Buddhism had it origins in India during the sixth century B.C. and takes its name from its founder, the Lord Buddha, the enlightened one. Buddha was the son of a chief of a people living in the foothills of the Himalayas who as a young man renounced ordinary life and the pursuit of wealth to practice asceticism and a wandering lifestyle. It is said that while living this way he gained the insight and wisdom that led to the development of the belief system that is the foundation of Buddhism. Much like Jesus Christ, Lord Buddha attracted many followers who maintained and propagated the beliefs he had espoused. During the third century B.C., Buddhist monks brought Buddhism to the Chao Phaya river basin in Thailand where it was adopted by the Mon people (Terwiel 1991). The first Buddhist monument in the region is located in what is today the city of Nakorn Pathom, about 40 miles west of Bangkok, and is said to be the largest Buddhist structure in the world. When the Tai people immigrated to the area they came to dominate the already established peoples, including the Mons, and adopted Buddhism from them. As we shall see, traditional Tai religious beliefs were blended with Buddhism to establish the religious beliefs and practices that persist as the religious dimension of Thai society (Suntaree 1991; Mulder 1994, Wyatt 1984, Keyes 1989).

Among scholars there is debate over whether Buddhism is primarily a philosophy or a religion. What is important for our purposes are the reasons for the debate. Although Buddhism recognizes the existence of supernatural beings, it is essentially **anthropocentric.** The religion is based on a rational analysis of the state of nature and the human condition, the consequences of each individual's actions, and the potential of each individual to achieve wisdom and perhaps ultimately enlightenment. Buddhism emphasizes knowledge and wisdom, or "right understanding," rather than belief. The debate therefore is predicated on the human emphasis of Buddhism and the lack of emphasis on supernatural beings as the means to change the human condition. But it is clear that Buddhism as a religion and philosophy of life presents a complex and sophisticated view of the metaphysical world and human nature. We now present an overview of the major elements of the religion that can help in understanding Thai society.

The starting point of Buddhist analysis is **dhamma** (dharma), the universal truth that has four major components, or "noble truths" (this account of Thai Buddhism is extracted from Walpoa 1988 and Khantipalo 1994). The first noble truth concerns the nature of existence for humans, which is the condition of suffering or unsatisfactoriness; human life is mainly unhappy. The second noble truth identifies the cause of this suffering, which is the great human delusion that happiness is to be found in the satisfaction of desire. Although humans can act out of either good or bad motives, unthinkingly they usually act on the basis of the bad, desires derived from greed, anger, jealousy, envy, hatred, selfishness, and so forth. Why does this lead to suffering? Because the world and human beings are always changing, the satisfaction of one desire just leads to another desire—that which is sought and obtained as satisfaction will change (e.g., a million dollars isn't what it once was). So humans get caught in the cycle of delusion, chasing happiness through the satisfaction of desires that are endless, and the objects of those desires are incapable of providing satisfaction. Notice that there is no great moral judgment inherent in this analysis of the human condition; instead, the focus is on human frailty and a lack of wisdom and insight.

   This leads to the third noble truth of Buddhist belief, the rational response to the condition of suffering: the processes made available by the laws of nature that provide relief from suffering. These involve knowing the dhamma, which means achieving understanding of one's condition and then changing what can be changed—the self, getting rid of delusion. Ultimately, since this is what is within the control of an individual, this means eliminating or overcoming desire, to eliminate the wanting in life. The fourth noble truth concerns the result or consequence of achieving right understanding, which is freedom from suffering. If one desires nothing then there is no unsatisfactoriness in life, no suffering. This is the state of enlightenment and bliss brought about by not being deluded and the absence of desire.

   In summary, Buddhism presents a rational response to the condition of suffering: Seek wisdom, understand the condition of suffering and its causes. From this understanding, it is clear that to experience happiness people must overcome the desires that are the cause of suffering or evil.

   Other key components of Buddhism are the concepts of samsara, kamma, and nibbana. **Samsara** refers to the cycle of birth, death, and reincarnation that is the essence of the impermanence of nature for living things. Humans are subject to this cycle and the suffering and unsatisfactoriness inherent in it. Buddhism provides not only the means for alleviation of suffering but the means for progress in the cycle of samsara and ultimately escape from it. **Kamma** (dharma) refers to the concept of conscious or willful action and the result or consequences of that action. What individuals decide to do, the actions over which they have control, have results in both the present life and in future reincarnations, and the accumulation of these effects are an individual's kamma. Bad actions create bad kamma, make people unhappy in this life, and can lead downward in the cycle of reincarnation. Conversely, good actions make people happy and satisfied in this life, will lead to a forward step in the cycle of reincarnation, and create good kamma. It is an absolute law of dhamma that every human action has its result or consequence. Finally, the state of enlightenment, first achieved by Buddha, and which all should seek to attain, is **nibbana,** or nirvana. It is the end of samsara, a permanent state of complete security and ultimate bliss since the sources of suffering, desire, hatred, and delusion have been extinguished.

   Together, the concepts of dhamma, kamma, samsara, and nibbana form the religious life view of the Thai Buddhist. Actions in past lives have determined one's place in the present, and actions in the present life will determine ones status in the next incarnation. The process is virtually infinite, but it is possible to attain the condition of enlightenment that ends the cycle. Good kamma is earned and suffering conquered through understanding achieved by practice.

   Buddhism lays out the means for doing this. Perhaps most important, Buddhism places the ability and responsibility for doing this on the individual. The Buddha was a teacher, not a savior or prophet; he was not divine but human; he "shows the way" but does not command. He achieved his enlightenment through his own efforts, not the grace of any deity. For the lay Buddhist, the beginning of countering the condition of suffering is found in following the five precepts.

Five Precepts of Buddhist Practice

1. I observe the precept of abstaining from the destruction of life.
2. I observe the precept of abstaining from taking that which is not given.
3. I observe the precept of abstaining from sexual misconduct.
4. I observe the precept of abstaining from falsehood.
5. I observe the precept of abstaining from intoxicants that cloud the mind and cause carelessness.

These precepts are a course of training willfully undertaken on a voluntary basis by the individual. Note the difference from Christianity and the 10 Commandments, which, according to belief, are given by God and state "thou shall not." Also, according to Buddhist thinking the precepts provide a moral foundation for society. On the social level they promote peaceful coexistence, mutual trust, a cooperative spirit, and general peace and harmony. More generally and positively there are the Buddhist virtues—kindness, compassion, and tolerance—which individuals can develop through appropriate practice and understanding. It must be emphasized that in Buddhist doctrine ritual adherence to the precepts is not the key; rather, the mental and spiritual state that leads to and is reinforced by Buddhist practice is essential.

THAI BUDDHISM IN EVERYDAY LIFE

For most lay Buddhists, and even most monks in Thailand, the achievement of nibbana in the present life is not an aspiration since it requires dedication beyond the ability of most people. Instead, good and bad kamma are operationalized in daily life as merit and demerit. Thai Buddhists seek to avoid actions that would have negative consequences causing one to lose merit; instead they try to think and act in ways that earn merit. Their goal is modest: to lead a satisfactory life and have good kamma for the next incarnation. It is in this context that Thai Buddhism emphasizes the value of moderation, the middle way. Even striving too hard to be a good Buddhist is a form of desire, the result of delusion. Emotionally, intellectually, and spiritually, it is better to be consistent, to avoid the extremes, not to expect too much of oneself, or life, for that matter. There are a wide variety of activities that gain merit, such as supporting the monkhood, renovating temples, practicing vegetarianism, participating in rituals, and, for some, meditating, as well as following the precepts.

Alms—An elderly woman places rice in the alms bowl of a Buddhist monk as he makes his early morning rounds. This practice is not considered "begging" by the monks, but instead an opportunity for the giver of food to gain merit or good kamma by supporting the Buddhist monkhood.

To understand the practice of religion in everyday Thai life, however, there is another element that must be considered. The ancient Thai religion or supernatural belief system is **animism,** the belief that as part of the natural order of things there are many spirits (*phii*) in the world. All over the world, preagricultural and early agricultural societies have had a strong tendency toward animist beliefs (Lenski, Lenski, and Nolan 1991), and especially so in Asia. Even as these societies developed to the advanced agricultural stage and then moved on to industrialization, animist beliefs persisted. In Thailand, the importance of these spirits stems from the fact that they are believed to have power: They can and do cause good and bad things to happen to people and communities (Mulder 1997).

An example that demonstrates the persistence of these beliefs is the prevalence of **spirit houses** throughout Thailand. Among the many types of spirits are the spirits or lords of physical places. Human occupancy of any place constitutes an infringement on such a spirit's rights. Thus, spirit houses, miniature houses in the traditional Thai style, are found at almost every Thai dwelling, temple, hotel, and office building, and even industrial parks. The purpose of the spirit house is to show recognition and respect for the spirit of the place. At the spirit house incense may be burned and offerings of food or flowers presented. As the existence and rights of the spirits are recognized, these spirits will not cause any mischief or suffering for the human occupants but instead offer their protection.

Just as there are spirits who are lords of the small spaces, there are spirits who are lords of the village or city, the province, and the nation.

There are also spirits of natural processes such as the growing of rice, the bringing of rain, fertility, and healing. All these spirits are both powerful within their domains and benign. They have no particular or innate hostility toward people, but they do have power and rights that must be respected. With knowledge people can manage their relationships with these spirits as in the example of the spirit houses or the performance of the proper ritual for bringing rain. As long as this type of spirit is treated correctly it will cause no harm and instead offer protection (Mulder 1997).

Often when asking a spirit for a wish to be fulfilled, the individual make a vow. The individual may offer to perform a certain ceremony or make a show of respect for the spirit in return for the granting of the favor. The spirit may be vengeful if the wish is granted and the vow not fulfilled. There is no moral dimension to relations with this type of spirit in these situations but rather a contract to be fulfilled. It is considered stupid or ignorant, not evil, to offend such a spirit.

In Thai animism there are other types of spirits that are not localized or attached to any particular natural process; instead, they roam and are evil. In human terms they are the source of chaos, misfortune, and disaster. Unlike the more neutral spirits described above, these do not necessarily act in response to how they are treated by people, are less subject to propitiation or manipulation, and may malevolently cause bad luck. These spirits have great power, and to counter them, a power greater than that of any normal individual or spirit is needed. The sources of great moral power, or goodness, with which to counter the evil spirits are some form of white magic, such as that brought on by Buddhist monks reciting incantations or spirit doctors. This good power can be concentrated in objects such as amulets, tatoos, or ritual formulas that protect one from the spirits. While the evil spirits can sometimes be paid off through very substantial gifts, there is no guarantee this will work. If all efforts to counter the effects of an evil spirit fail, all one can do is endure until the spirit moves on. Ultimately, it is the Buddhist monk, closely aligned with the goodness and virtue of the Buddha and dhamma who is the agent best able to vanquish these evil spirits.

Most important in understanding religion in everyday life in Thailand is to recognize how Buddhist and animist beliefs combine. Religion in Thailand is therefore based upon a continuum from moral goodness to evil power (Mulder 1994: 41–60). Ultimate goodness is defined in terms of Buddhism and the stability, predictability, and wisdom embodied in it. It is the source of order and security in an uncertain and threatening life environment. At the other end of the continuum, ultimate power and evil are defined by the condition of chaos and danger in the realm of the roaming, harmful spirits. Next to the moral goodness of Buddhism is that of the family, particularly the mother, giver of life, unconditional love, and security. Moving closer to the realm of power there is the domain of the community. Here again order is provided but not necessarily love, and the individual is less secure and more subject to forces beyond his or her control. Then there is the domain of those spirits who can be comprehended and managed to prevent harm. Finally, there is the domain of chaos and disorder, the bad spirits who are always dangerous and threatening (Mulder 1994). The merging of these sets of beliefs, animist and Buddhist, comprises what can be called the **popular Buddhism** that most Thais practice.

There are approximately 30,000 Buddhist temples in Thailand and over 200,000 monks and 100,000 novices. In almost any city or village one will find orange-robed monks on the streets in the early morning accepting gifts of food from women. This ritual provides an opportunity for the giver to gain merit and the monks to provide their daily sustenance. The temples have been the organizing institutions of most communities as they have been the centers not only of religious life but education, health care, rituals, and community meetings. As development proceeds and the government provides specialized agencies, these functions of the temple are being displaced while the more distinctly religious functions remain. The temples are the sites of rituals and festivals, which are Buddhist and animist.

One of the most important of these rituals is the death ritual where monks are responsible for guiding the deceased out of the realm of chaos and into a better life, while at the same time safeguarding the peace of the living. However, at most temples in Thailand one will also find fortune-telling, lotteries, and the sale of amulets and charms to ward off evil spirits. As the exemplification of goodness, the temples and the monks associated with them provide the basis of security and contentment for the community.

Other evidence of the prevalence of Buddhist belief is the many images of Buddha one finds throughout Thailand and all other Buddhist countries in Asia. They are found not only in the many temples but in homes, cars, trucks, and offices. According to strict Buddhist belief, the images are not the Buddha but representations that can be used to achieve greater concentration on practice or as point of focus for reflection and meditation. The images are deserving of respect, which is shown by bowing or obeisance. In popular Buddhism the images are often treated as sacred. Some images are believed to have special powers or magic with regard to healing or the granting of wishes.

According to Buddhist doctrine, such beliefs are mere superstition, not rational; they are misunderstandings stemming from blind faith and false hope with no basis in Buddhist teaching. These superstitions offer no escape from suffering as there is in dhamma. However, wishes based on wisdom and without selfish motives may be made before any image or object that represents noble ideals and virtues. These are positive resolutions for wholesome actions and may be necessary for the accomplishment of appropriate goals.

It would not be at all unusual to find the headliner of a car bearing Buddhist inscriptions applied by a monk in a ceremony of blessing to protect the occupants in their travels. Similarly many vehicles, including government vehicles and the airplanes of the national airline, have been blessed and bear Buddha images or other sacred charms. It is common even for well-educated and successful Thais to wear amulets and images as protection from evil spirits. As shown on the cover photo, a good example of all this is the Erawan Shrine, located on a street corner in one of the busiest sections of Bangkok, in front of a large Japanese department store, across from the huge World Trade Center, and across another street from the newly opened Planet Hollywood, with the new elevated commuter train going overhead. The little Erawan Shrine is normally crowded with people daily offering gifts of elephant statues, garlands of flowers, or food to the spirit believed to be present there. The shrine has a permanent troupe of traditional dancers who will dance for a fee to redeem a vow or obtain the spirit's good favor. And it is common for university students to visit this shrine as well as others on their campus to obtain good fortune on examinations (Majapuria 1993).

What is most important to remember is that Buddhist and animist beliefs infuse life in Thailand. The pursuit, or at least recognition, of merit and the existence and propitiation of spirits are part of the magical normal order of things, as natural to Thais as breathing, eating, and drinking.

THE ORGANIZATION OF BUDDHISM IN THAILAND

Buddhism is closely aligned with the state in Thailand. At the time of the Ayudhyan period of Thai history examined in Chapter 2, *Brahmanic* elements from the Indian Hindu religion were added to the notion of kingship, making the kings a type of deity. During the drive for modernization begun in the 1850s, Thai monarchs and the elite harnessed Buddhism as a unifying principle of society and a legitimator of monarchic power in a time of transition (Somboon 1993). Today Buddhism is officially sponsored by the government as one of the three major elements of Thai identity, the others being king and country. Historically and at present the king is the patron of the **Sangha** (organized priesthood) and appoints the patriarchs at its head. But there are many other ways that the state supports Buddhism.

The constitution mandates that the king be a Buddhist, by custom he performs certain religious rituals, and monks are participants in state celebrations and rituals. The authoritative translation and specification of Buddhist texts is carried out under the sponsorship of the government. Ecclesiastical laws are set by the government as are the religious and secular curriculums in the temple schools. Buddhism is also a component of the curriculum in the government schools, with emphasis on the elements of Buddhism that support the established order: the perpetuation of values, good citizenship, respect for the social order, with an emphasis on form and ritual rather than deeper topics of belief and practice.

The Sangha, or formal priesthood, is not a force for change but an upholder of the status quo. At its lower levels it is quite tolerant and liberal, as is Buddhism generally, but within the hierarchy it is very stratified, conservative, and dominated by the elders. It reflects the hierarchical and stratified nature of Thai society, and its structure parallels the civil service with grades, ranks, and titles (Mulder 1997).

There are probably about 30,000 monks in the Sangha making monkhood their career. Most monks, however, are not seeking advancement in the hierarchy and are content to fulfill the role of spiritual and ritual leader and personal adviser to the people in the community of the temple. In this way these men can become respected local notables. And there is, of course, a small minority of monks who have sought to adapt the monk's traditional role to the modern era. They provide leadership in community organizations, encourage the community to press their rights and demands on the government, sponsor local development projects, and sometimes articulate an ethical basis for environmental concerns. To date these activities are not the route to promotion within the Sangha and the ranks and titles that come with it.

RELIGION IN THAILAND: A CONCLUSION

It is important to emphasize again that Thai people take religion quite seriously. Walking through the big cities of Thailand as well as in the countryside, one continues to see most Thais paying their respect to their religion by following important rituals such as putting their hands together in a wai when passing a temple or other important religious site, giving alms to monks, and treating them with extensive reverence (such as by following rules specifying that women do not touch monks and can hand them objects only if they are placed on a tray first). Though it is in some decline, the practice of having all young men enter the mookhood for a period of time, continues. Over 80 to 90 percent of young men continue to do so, a quite remarkable number when comparing modern Thailand to other countries, in the West or Asia, with similar levels of economic development.

Many Thais claim that their traditional respect for the moral principles of Buddhism, along with the religious training almost all young men receive as temporary monks, has kept the nation's social problems, such as crime, lower than they would otherwise be. But as in all developing societies, there will no doubt be a drop in religiosity among the average Thai person as education and the economy expand. It seems, however, that religion in Thailand will remain stronger than in most nations far after extensive economic development has been obtained.

CHAPTER 7

The Family and Education in Thailand

One of our closest friends in Thailand grew up in a small southern village. As he tells it, unlike fathers of rural origins often say, his little village *was not* five miles from the city, but rather five miles to the *nearest road* to get to the city! When our friend was growing up, as with all people living in a peasant society, his family was an all-powerful influence on his life, and family obligations remained extremely strong throughout life. Still today, while in his 50s and living and working in the big city (and all over the world), his extended family has remained very strong, continuing to provide material and psychological help to all extended family members in need, as is the case in the vast majority of Thai families today. As is typical in Thailand, for example, if the daughter of a distant cousin in a village far from Bangkok has won a scholarship to attend an exclusive high school in Bangkok, it goes without question that these family members in Bangkok will take her into their home and care for her like a mother and father while she lives in the big city. While Thais may be rather independent people compared to most other Asians, as noted in our first chapter, this independence does not take away from the family as being the most important group in the society.

Our old friend provides us with another example of key aspects of old peasant Thai society and urban Thailand today. When he was a young child living in the jungle village, there were only very limited opportunities for education. In villages like his maybe just a couple of years of education would be provided by the local Buddhist monks of the village. In such a peasant society, education obtained from outside the family is rare and seldom needed; the mental and technical skills required in life can be obtained within the family. Unlike the vast majority of village children his age, however, our friend received higher education. The monks of his village recognized his talent, sponsored him for a scholarship to an elite high school in Bangkok, where he was accepted and graduated with top scores. From there he won scholarships to the most prestigious Thai university, then one in England, and finally one that allowed him to achieve a Ph.D. at Stanford University in California. The Thailand of our friend today is a society of modern industries and rapid economic growth, as we have already seen. Our friend's professional services are in great demand because one of the major problems in Thailand today is, in fact, a severe shortage of skilled and educated people to run the modern economy and governmental agencies required of a developing society.

Of the two social **institutions** considered in this chapter, the family has been by far the most important throughout the history of human societies around the world. So important and basic is the family to human societies that sociologists refer to it as the *master institution*. When we examine the history of human societies, from hunting and gathering societies to today's modern postindustrial societies, we find that all societies, in every age and world region, have had the institution of the family (Lenski, Lenski, and Nolan 1991).

More than 10,000 years ago, when all people existed in some kind of hunting and gathering society, the family was in fact the only institution. This is why the family can be referred to as the master institution. In these early societies, the family system or clan did it all: The clan served the functions of a political system, with elders perhaps acting as leaders; an economic system, with a division of labor within the family working to supply basic necessities; and a quasi-religious system, with elders perhaps acting as spiritual advisers and passing on the myths of the clan origins. It was not until simple settled agriculture developed less than 10,000 years ago that the other institutions slowly became distinguished as separate subsystems within the society. In fact, education, the other institution considered in this chapter, did not become a separate institution until more advanced or modern societies appeared. Until that time, the family could still be relied upon to teach young people all they needed to know to be competent adults in the society. With so much more technical information needed by those hoping to move into advanced societies, the separate institution of education had to exist.

In this chapter we will begin with the Thai family system and its primary characteristics. Finally we will turn to the educational system in Thailand and its rapid change today.

THE FAMILY IN THAILAND

When examining the family as an institution it is necessary to distinguish between the concepts of family and household. *Household* is an empirical concept defined as the occupants of a dwelling who engage in some measure of cooperative activity on a regular basis. The **family,** however, is a more subjective cultural concept comprising the meaning members of a society give to the idea of family. When households meet the subjective definition of family, the concepts coincide; however, those two concepts may diverge greatly when what people think of as family is significantly different from the household. Certainly households change over time, and more slowly does the cultural subjective definition of family—neither concept is completely static. In Thailand the basic definition of a family is that of a modified **extended family,** which includes grandparents, parents, children, and others related by kinship.

When the family is examined from the perspective of the household (those living in one physical space), the most common type in Thailand is the **nuclear family,** consisting of husband, wife, and unmarried children. The second most common type is the extended family in which grandparents are also present. A recent study indicates that about 61 percent of the households in Thailand are nuclear, a little over 23 percent are vertical extended families, 9 percent extended families, and 6 percent one-person households. According to the 1990 census, average household size has dropped to 4.4 persons compared to 5.2 in 1980. Household size is largest in the northeast with an average of 4.7, while in Bangkok it is 4.1 (Bhasshorn 1995).

These statistics, however, mask the dynamics of family development, which generally occurs in a three-stage cycle. The choice of a starting point in the cycle is arbitrary, but let the nuclear family be the first stage. In the second stage a newly married child and spouse form a subunit in the household, creating a small extended family. In contrast to the Western world, and most of Asia as well, the most common pattern in Thailand has been **matrilocal residence** (in contrast to **patrilocal residence**), as a newly married couple takes residence in the bride's parents' home where they will live until they have a child or until another of the children in the original nuclear family gets married, after which the couple that married first leaves the family to establish their own nuclear household. The third stage occurs as the last of the children marries. In Thailand this is usually the youngest daughter, and she and her spouse will stay with the parents to take care of them during old age. Typically, this child inherits the house and its contents upon the death of the parents.

This family cycle generates a variety of subjective definitions as to when a new family is established—at marriage, upon separation of residence from parents, or with separate residence and children from the marital relationship. In general then, a family is the parents and children, with some other relatives, usually grandparents, present for at least part of the family's life. Families are horizontally and vertically extended since other relatives, such as aunts and uncles often live in the same community within relatively close proximity. It is a feature of extended family life in Thailand that aunts, uncles, cousins, nephews, and nieces tend to stay in touch and regularly visit each other, perform mutual favors, and enjoy the security of extensive family contacts.

Outside of Bangkok it is common for extended families to live in a compound with separate dwellings for nuclear households but to practice extended family life in daily interactions of a social nature and occasional cooperative group activity. Matrilocal residence after marriage in Thailand is not only the most common pattern of family development but appears to be increasing in frequency. In one study, 37.8 percent of men reported living with their spouse's parents, while 28.3 percent lived with their own parents after marriage. Among women, 56.2 percent reported living with their own parents and only 18.7 percent with the male spouse's parents. At least two-thirds of all married couples live for a time with the parents of one spouse (Chai 1994). In urban areas **neolocal residence**—the newly married couple establishing their own residence—is most common; it is less common in rural areas. In the urban south, Bangkok, and the central region, the most common alternative is patrilocal residence, where the newly married couple lives with the husband's parents. This is a reflection of Chinese influence as these are the areas with the largest proportion of ethnic Chinese people. Matrilocal residence is most common in the north, northeastern rural areas, and urban areas other than those mentioned for patrilocal residence. These patterns of postnuptial residence have remained fairly stable over time as their frequency has increased (Chai 1994, Bhasshorn 1995). By age 50, over 75 percent of married couples have established independent households.

The authority structure within Thai families is usually based on age and gender, with the senior male viewed as the head of the family, while the senior female exercises authority in the absence of the senior male. Survey data show that about two-thirds of the respondents agreed with a statement asserting that a husband should have authority over his wife. These divisions of authority, however, are not rigid; in actual practice most major family decisions are reached on the basis of consultation between the husband and wife, but other senior family members may also participate. The husband has greater external responsibility and represents the family outside the home, while the woman exercises internal authority within the home. As in the overall hierarchy of Thai society, the elderly are awarded the highest status within the family and are consulted for their wisdom and advice on a wide range of matters. Both husband and wife are expected to take responsibility for child rearing, as is in fact the common practice. While most Thai men are actively engaged in bringing up children, women do carry a greater responsibility within the home due to traditional sex roles and because they tend to work fewer hours outside the home (Bhasshorn 1994; Bhasshorn et al. 1995).

As is the pattern in most traditional societies, in Asia and the West, in rural Thailand the extended family is the fundamental social and economic unit and has a variety of functions and forms. All able-bodied members of a family are expected to contribute economically by providing labor for farm production, supplementary wage-earning activity, or both. The family performs further economic functions by providing training in farming and homemaking as well as by launching careers. The emphasis on all family members contributing is reflected in the Thai labor force, of which women make up over 44 percent. Females are more likely to participate in work outside of the household in the rural sector, where over 75 percent are employed, compared to urban areas where the rate is about 58 percent (Bhasshorn 1995). Again focusing on rural Thailand, the emphasis on work is demonstrated by the age at which gainful employment begins, primarily in agriculture: at around 11 years of age for women and 12 for men. When compared to industrial societies all over the world, these figures lend support to the assertion that childhood as a stage in the life cycle meant for play and social development is a new concept only affordable generally in developed nations or among the affluent in the less developed nations.

Male and female children in Thailand are treated equally in most respects. Although there is a modest preference for male children, it is not as strong as in most of East and Southeast Asia. Education is provided by the government but still has substantial costs for a family, and many children obtain only a minimal six years of education. Again in contrast to most of Asia, Thai parents believe that if family resources limit the number of children who can be educated, the resources should support the education of the most talented child regardless of gender.

Thai families also provide for children through inheritance, and the traditional pattern is of equal shares going to all children regardless of age or gender, with the notable exception of leaving more to the child who looks after the parents during old age (usually the youngest female child) (Chai 1994; Bhasshorn et al. 1995). In one study, among respondents whose parents' property had been divided, over 70 percent reported the divisions had been equal to all children. In the rural northeast, however, where postnuptial matrilocal residence is most common, daughters receive larger shares of inheritance, usually in land, than sons. The physical proximity is maintained by matrilocal residence, and it may establish stronger emotional bonds between parents and daughters compared to those with sons. The equal share tradition, however, may be changing as rural families provide higher levels of education to some children with the resulting ability to earn nonfarm income. In these instances the children with more education receive smaller shares than those with less. Inheritance of farmland is a process where children are first given the right to use the land, often while living with the parents. After establishing their own household, the children continue to work the land without legal title. When the parents get quite old they grant legal rights to the land to each of the children.

As is the case all over the world, the Thai family is the primary means of socializing the young with the values of the society. There are four areas that have been identified as the major focus of children's learning within the Thai family: religion, hierarchy, sex roles, and obligations to parents. It is in the family that children receive most of their attachment to Buddhism and learn the concepts of merit and demerit in the context of kamma. Children also begin learning the hierarchical nature of Thai society within families, which have their own hierarchical structure. The family system is based on superordinate-subordinate relationships, and one of the most important of these is age ranking, with the senior deserving great reverence. The family also instills respect for superordinate-subordinate relationships among relatives, as well as toward teachers, monks, government officials, and many others. Concomitant with learning the existence of hierarchy and one's place in it, children learn the importance of respect for everyone. The Thai hierarchy is based not only on rank but also on the concept of respect. In the family, children learn that all members, and by extension all individuals in society, are deserving of respect and that every individual may expect to receive respect in social interactions.

Thai children, as elsewhere, also learn sex roles within the family. Women's roles are defined in terms of child care, care for the elderly, housework, and income-generating activities. The family is conceptually centered on women, although they have less formal power than men, and the concept of women as the givers of life, combined with the Buddhist belief in reincarnation, creates an almost mystical idea of the mother as the source of goodness and security. Male roles are directed toward the world outside the family where they are expected to provide for material needs and increase the status, prestige, and respect of the family.

One of the most important socializing functions of the Thai family is with regard to the obligation children have toward their parents. The parent-child relationship is a bunkhun relationship, the belief that children are expected to be grateful toward parents and to demonstrate this gratefulness. Daughters carry a greater responsibility than sons for the care of parents, and there is evidence that a substantial majority of Thais believe that a woman's duty to her parents and parents-in-law should take precedence over her duty to her husband. The elderly are more likely to prefer the care of a daughter in old age over that of a son. Equally pervasive is the belief that elderly parents should live with a child's family, again preferably a daughter. Sons also have obligations and are expected to provide financial support and to gain merit for parents. The ritual ordination as monks that most men undergo for a short period (as noted in the previous chapter) is one means of gaining merit for the family, and all children are expected to make merit for deceased parents (Bhasshorn 1994).

Marriage in Thailand

In Western cultures, with greater individualism, less emphasis on extended family ties, and higher levels of economic development, romantic love is generally a prerequisite for marriage, which is primarily seen as a means of personal fulfillment. In cultures with lower levels of economic development and a more collective orientation (as noted for Asian nations in our first chapter), extended family ties are more important and romantic love is much less important in marriage decisions. Thus, in Thailand, as in most Asian countries, romantic love is not the most important factor in choosing a marriage partner. Instead, the compatibility of a potential partner with both the individual and the family receives great emphasis. The institution of marriage is seen as providing social rather than personal fulfillment through the security and status attained and the opportunity to perform meaningful social roles. It provides women the opportunity to perform the important social roles of mother and head of domestic household and men the role of provider and head representative of the household in the broader social context. Attitudes regarding the relative lesser importance of romantic love in Asian nations are also reflected in attitudes regarding divorce, where the absence of love is not viewed as a sufficient reason for terminating a marriage. As Thailand develops and becomes more exposed to Western cultural norms, notions of romantic love are becoming more accepted and views regarding marriage are gradually changing (Levine, et al. 1995).

Exact rates of marriage and divorce are difficult to ascertain in Thailand, but survey data indicate that marriage is almost universal as practically all Thais are married at some time in their lives (Bhasshorn 1995; Bhasshorn et al. 1995). While the Thai family law of 1935 requires that a marriage be registered with the government to be fully legal, in rural areas it is very common that marriages are not registered. The community views an unregistered union as a formal marriage provided there is some public declaration through a formal and elaborate ceremony, religious ritual, or informal announcement that a couple is living together.

The average age of marriage for women is over 22 years, though there are regional disparities resulting from social, cultural, and economic factors. In Bangkok the average age of first marriage for women is almost 26 years, while it is 23.4 years in the surrounding central region. In the north the average is 22 years, while it is 21.9 in the south and 21.6 in the northeast (Bhasshorn 1995). These rates coincide with the relative wealth and levels of education in the regions, with marriage occurring earlier where income and education are lower. Age of first marriage for men follows the same pattern, but they tend to marry later by several years.

The tradition in many parts of Thailand regarding mate selection was arranged marriage, with parents choosing a child's spouse. But during the 20th century this pattern had changed, and since the 1960s free

choice of the individuals concerned has become the norm. Parental approval, though, remains an important factor in mate selection, and fairly
recent data indicate that a majority of both men and women would delay
or forgo marriage if they did not receive this approval. However, men
are less likely to follow this practice than women (Bhasshorn 1994).

Generally, as is the case in most traditional societies, people in
Thailand marry within rather than between social strata, and the ability
of a potential spouse to get along well with the other's family is an important criterion of selection. Women usually marry men older than
themselves, but it is not unusual for men to marry older women. Also in
Thailand, following a matrilineal pattern, it is customary for the groom
to give gifts of money to the bride and the bride's parents before marriage. The gift to the bride provides some guarantee of stability and security to her, and the gift to the parents is given in respect, is recognition of
their efforts at raising their daughter, signifies approval of the marriage,
and contributes to the process of integrating the groom into the bride's
family. In normal practice these gifts are both symbolic and functional
and are not extravagant. Most people support the practice but think the
gifts should reflect what the groom and his family can reasonably afford.

As with marriage, exact rates of marriage dissolution through separation and divorce are not known, but it is clearly a frequent occurrence
with estimates for dissolution of all marriages ranging between 8 and
20 percent. The legal divorce rate pertaining to registered marriages is increasing; it is estimated that for women as many as 20 percent of first
marriages are dissolved within 15 years, and after 20 years the rate is
25 percent. The divorce rate is highest in Bangkok and the more economically developed areas and lowest in rural areas. Remarriage is common,
with younger women under age 25 demonstrating a remarriage rate of
80 percent within five years of dissolution and women over 25 a 50 percent
rate within five years. Survey data indicate that only about 25 percent of
the population oppose in principle the remarriage of divorced women.

Overall, most Thais seem quite satisfied with their married lives. It
is important in making this generalization to reinforce the social rather
than personal nature of marriage. There are indications that men are
more satisfied than women, as over 40 percent of men in one study responded that they were very satisfied and over 50 percent moderately
satisfied. Among women, less than 25 percent responded that they were
very satisfied, but slightly more than 70 percent were moderately satisfied. Still, this means that less than 5 percent of both men and women
were less than satisfied with their marriages (Chai 1994).

One final note on marriage concerns the practice of **polygamy.**
Until passage of the 1935 marriage law, men could have multiple wives.
Today men may have only one legal wife, but since unregistered unions
are viewed as legitimate the practice of polygamy persists in the form of
minor wives. If a man fulfills the function of husband with a woman

other than his legal wife she is viewed by others and the couple perceives themselves as married (Bhasshorn 1995). The functions of husband include not only sexual union but financial support and establishing a son-in-law relationship with the woman's family. It is impossible to estimate the frequency of multiple marriages of this type, but clearly the practice continues, especially in urban areas among the more affluent.

The Future of the Family in Thailand: A Conclusion

The family is in a state of change and transition as Thailand develops. As urbanization and industrialization proceed, the extended nature of the Thai family system is changing to the nuclear. Members of families immigrate to the cities in search of work, and intimate family bonds are difficult to sustain. Young people desire higher-paying nonfarm jobs and are able to obtain them (Akin 1993). This provides a variety of freedoms, including less dependence on parents and inheritance for economic security and consequently less parental control of young people.

As population growth has slowed and there are fewer children per couple, children's obligations to parents become more difficult to fulfill. Modern agencies, such as government welfare agencies, perform many of the functions formerly provided by extended families, both contributing to the further weakening of the family's importance and as a response to it. In the cities a youth culture is also developing, in contrast to rural villages where children are constrained by the system of familial and personal social relationships surrounding them. At a minimum, in the rural areas what children do will almost always become known to their parents and there are many adults to provide guidance. In the cities children are more anonymous, delay work for education, have more free time, and receive money from their parents. As a result, they can engage in activity independent of parental control and knowledge. More and more young people do not agree with or follow the practice of giving respect and submission to the elderly.

Previously we have pointed out the universality of marriage in Thailand. With economic development, attitudes and reality regarding marriage and the family are changing, especially for women, as the newly industrializing and modernizing economy provides the opportunity for economic security outside of marriage. People are now more likely to delay marriage for educational and economic opportunities, and it is even more common to forgo marriage altogether. Remaining single, greater equality and authority for women in the family, and teenagers making more decisions for themselves are results of modern attitudes; and the factor having the greatest impact on these attitudes is education, as the more educated are more likely to hold these views. Men tend to have more modern attitudes than women except that they are less likely to support remarriage of women after divorce and more likely to oppose the idea of men doing more kitchen work, or any housework. The northeast is the region most traditional regarding the family and traditional family values. Finally, as is typical of modernization, most people think the government will have to play a greater role in the care of the elderly in the future as there is recognition that it will be less feasible for children to provide all of their parents' needs (Bhasshorn 1994; Bhasshorn et al. 1995).

EDUCATION IN THAILAND

Educational systems all over Asia have many similarities. Early in the morning, each weekday (and for many more weeks out of the year than in the United States), children can be seen in their school uniforms heading off to school. The uniforms, of course, differ from country to country in Asia, and from school to school in Thailand, but all schools require uniforms. One of the central goals of most Asian educational systems is to promote group cooperation and conformity; school uniforms are considered essential in promoting this goal. In Thailand it is usually a dark-colored skirt and white blouse for girls and a white shirt and brown or dark-blue slacks for boys. Even university students often wear uniforms, at least for the first two years, and they take pride in attaching their university's pin to their shirt or blouse. (As we will see below, getting into a top university in Thailand is very difficult, which makes it understandable that students want to show off the uniform and school pin.)

The Formal Organization of Thai Education

Once these students all over Asia reach their classrooms there are again many similarities. Most of these similarities are due to the fact that many Asian countries copied the basic format of American primary and secondary education earlier in the 20th century (Rohlen 1982). Seventy-five to 100 years ago, the United States showed the world how to succeed with education for the masses of people when countries in Europe still held to the idea of education only for the upper classes. (In most respects, of course, the rest of the world today no longer sees the American primary and secondary educational system as the model to follow.) Thus, there are 6 years of basic primary education in Thailand; middle schools and high schools bring education up to 12 years.

Under new laws passed in the mid-1990s, all children in Thailand are now required to attend at least 9 years of school. Before this time it was only 6 years, and soon in the 21st century all children will be required to attend 12 years of schooling as in the more developed countries of Asia such as Japan, South Korea, and Taiwan. By 1980, already 90 percent of the Thai population was literate, though only 9 percent finished high school (Keyes 1989: 145–146). In the mid-1990s, the United Nations' International Labor Organization estimated that only 16 percent of Thai children between the ages of 10 and 14 were working and not in school, a percentage lower than most of Thailand's neighbors (*Bangkok Post*, December 11, 1997). But Thailand's goal is to have 95 percent of all young people graduating from high school by the year 2000 (Pasuk and Baker 1996a: 107). As we will see in more detail below, Thailand is in the midst of extensive educational expansion, with hundreds of new schools and dozens of new junior colleges being built so the country can face the new challenge of global economic competition (Muscat 1994: 239–40).

Quality of Thai Education

Once we get past the formal organization of Asian educational institutions, however, the similarities to the United States fall away quickly. The biggest differences are found in their methods of learning, how long they attend school, the amount of work they are required to complete, the centralization and standardization of school systems, and the high level of respect directed toward teachers at all levels of education.

International comparisons of how much Asian teenagers know compared to their North American and European counterparts always put young people from a number of Asian countries on top, with Thai young people scoring about equal to those in the other Asian countries (Shapiro 1992: 66; Kerbo and McKinstry 1998). In fact, American high school seniors score toward the bottom in standardized tests of math and science when compared to same-age students all over Europe and Asia.[5] There are many reasons for the low American scores and high Asian scores, such as the fewer days a year Americans attend school, less emphasis put on education by parents in the United States, the American youth subculture that tends to be anti-intellectual and puts down students who have high academic achievement (those people are often considered "nerds"), and the amount of money American schools spend on athletics rather than academics. But more than anything else, comparative research indicates it is the amount of work given to each student, and the introduction of difficult subjects at an earlier age to Asian children compared to American children, that makes most of the difference. (A few years ago both authors once talked with two Thai teenage girls who had just returned from four years in the United States where their parents were studying for Ph.D.s at an American university. We asked them what they most missed about the United States and were told "pizza." We can note that they must now be happier because their city west of Bangkok now has a Pizza Hut as of 1997. We then asked what they most disliked about being back in Thailand and were told quite strongly, "the homework.")

Asian primary and secondary schools—especially in Japan, South Korea, Taiwan, and Thailand—focus on cramming their students' heads with massive amounts of facts and figures, using what is often referred to as rote learning, or memorization. One primary purpose of education in these Asian countries is to help students pass the extremely difficult and competitive college entrance examinations at the end of their high school careers.

For this type of system to work in Thailand and other Asian countries, it also requires extensive centralization of school systems. In a major contrast to the United States, in most Asian countries a Ministry of Education has almost complete control over what is taught in primary and secondary schools, how it is taught, and at what age it is taught. The Ministry of Education continually conducts reviews of subjects taught in the schools, and if deemed necessary it will revise extensive lesson plans and require teachers to use them. This was done during 1998 for the subject of environmental issues in Thailand.

While students from these Asian educational systems learn more about subjects such as math and science compared to the average American student, there is a major drawback to the Asian educational system— lack of creativity and critical thinking. The emphasis on memorization or rote learning gets the facts into young heads, but it does not promote what can be called creative thinking. Studies have shown that Thai students are not given information allowing for critical thinking, especially with respect to questions about Thai history and the moral order of their society (Mulder 1997). And in a world where economic competition is becoming more based on knowledge industries (computers, biotechnology, for example), the lack of creativity and critical thinking puts Asian nations such as Thailand behind in the race. These countries are aware of the problem and are now starting to consider how they can redesign educational programs to promote more creativity among their students, but there is yet no evidence suggesting they will be able to achieve their desired results.

Universities

The university system in Thailand is more similar to that in the United States, but again there are some important exceptions. Two are related to the importance of achieving a top university degree for one's future. These differences are also related to how students are admitted to universities and the distinct ranking of universities in terms of status and supposed quality. We will consider this last characteristic first.

Top-ranked universities in the United States include Harvard, Princeton, Yale, University of California at Berkeley, Stanford, and so forth. Achieving a degree from one of these universities, of course, gives a boost to future career achievements. But there is still the chance of

moving to the top of one's profession in the United States having graduated from one of the lesser-ranked universities. This is much less the case
in Thailand and other Asian nations. In Thailand, Chulalongkorn University is clearly rated at the top, with a small number of others such as
Thammasat, Mahidol, Silpakorn, and Prince of Songkla Universities just
below. A much greater percentage of top business executives, lawyers,
architects, and other professionals in Thailand have graduated from top-
ranked universities than is the case in the United States.

It is of course quite difficult to gain admission to one of these top
universities in Thailand as a student; it requires high scores on a very
rigorous college entrance examination. However, once admitted it requires much less money to attend than it does in the United States
(*Bangkok Post*, October 24, 1997). To be admitted to Chulalongkorn University in Thailand, for example, the admission requirements are focused
primarily on the one entrance exam. There are many cases of bribes
given, what is commonly called "tea money" in Thailand, to help obtain
admission to a college, but this has been found primarily to occur in
small, less prestigious colleges and universities in Thailand (*The Nation*,
June 4, 1998). Thus, when it comes to the most respected universities,
how much money your parents have is only significant in the extra tutoring they can buy that will help the student achieve a higher score on the
entrance exam. And because of the importance of getting into a good
university in Thailand, this extra tutoring is becoming a big business.
Much like parents in Japan who send their children to after-hours
schools or cram schools called *juku* (Rohlen 1982; Kerbo and McKinstry
1998), Thai parents with money are willing to spend much of it on sending their children to such a school that will improve their chances of getting into a good university (*Bangkok Post*, July 20, 1996).

In line with what has been described for high schools in Asia, we
can say that the best and the brightest achieve admission to the top universities in Thailand, that is, the best and brightest in memorizing massive amounts of information so as to pass the written exams for college
entrance. Again there are questions about creativity and intellectual in-
novation instilled in those students given the method of selection for the
universities. It is quite likely that many of the innovative minds at Micro-
soft's research lab in Washington state, for example, would not have
been accepted into the top universities in Asia when they were younger.
We will take up this issue again when considering the importance of education for economic development in our next section.

Education for Economic Development

It is clear that throughout the 20th century investments in education
have produced the basis for economic expansion (Walters and Rubinson
1983). As the 20th century draws to a close, it is even more clear that

education is critical for a competitive economy in the face of the importance of new high-tech industries. In the past, Thailand was able to compete in the world economy with its advantage in cheap labor and raw materials, especially agriculture. But those days for Thailand are numbered. Behind Thailand is Laos, Vietnam, Burma, and other countries moving into the world economy with even cheaper labor and raw materials. Thus, while cheap labor and raw materials have moved Thailand's economy to its present stage, to move further and increase the standard of living for Thai citizens, Thailand must move into more high-tech industries (Country Profile, World Bank, www.worldbank.com, January 1998).

Understanding all of the above, Thailand has set government policy to greatly expand education in coming decades. Elementary and secondary education will be greatly expanded, and the minimum years of schooling required by law will soon be 12 instead of 6 (Pasuk and Baker 1996a: 96). Even more educational expansion is occurring with respect to postsecondary education, however. For example, the 36-campus Rajabhat Institute, which was similar to a large junior college system all over Thailand, is now being upgraded to a university system using the 23-campus California State University system as a model (*Bangkok Post*, January 6, 1998). Millions of dollars in loans and tax money have gone into sending current Rajabhat faculty overseas to update their education and improve teaching at the Rajabhat Institute. Further, the Department of Vocational Education (DOVE) in the Ministry of Education has expanded the current junior college and technical college system and will be adding dozens of new campuses in coming years.[6] And finally, there is much more investment coming to existing universities such as Chulalongkorn, Thammasat, Mahidol, and Silpakorn. For example, the size of Silpakorn's larger campus in Nakorn Pathom has almost doubled; its engineering college has expanded from 700 students to 2,000.

Education in Thailand: A Conclusion

As we have already seen, education was first expanded dramatically under the reign of King Chulalongkorn in the late 1800s (Girling 1981). Much like in Japan with its Meiji Restoration during the same period (Kerbo and McKinstry 1998), it was the establishment of modern education at the time that helped propel Thailand from a weak little feudal kingdom into the dynamic and growing economy it became, especially by the 1980s. But it is clear that Thailand is now stuck in an economic status that will not bring rapid improvements as in the past unless education further expands. As noted in beginning the current set of chapters on basic institutions, as societies modernize and become more complex in the industrial and postindustrial ages, institutions such as education and science emerge to be as important as the institutions that first played central roles in societies: the family, religion, politics, and the economy.

With the slowdown of the Thai economy and financial crisis in the late 1990s, there are questions about how quickly Thailand can expand its educational institutions to take up the new world challenge, or even if it can expand them at all. Some of the loans from the World Bank worth several millions of U.S. dollars earmarked for educational expansion, for example, had to be returned unspent (*Bangkok Post*, January 11, 1998). Most agree, however, that the economic crisis of the late 1990s will prove to be only a setback in Thailand's drive for educational expansion and modernization: There is no choice for Thailand but to upgrade educational institutions if it is to continue to compete in the new world economy.

CHAPTER 8

Social Change
and Social Problems
in Modern Thailand

Economic development and modernization are always painful processes for any society to experience. This was the case a few hundred years ago when European countries were the first to industrialize, and it continues to be so today. Economic development brings dislocation: There is rapid urbanization that disrupts families and traditional lifestyles, people are torn away from old communities of support, and religious institutions can no longer be relied upon for the security they once provided. One of the most destabilizing features of industrialization is the rapid migration of a large proportion of the peasant population into the urban areas. Some of this migration is the result of what demographers call the *push factor,* that is, it becomes more difficult for peasant families to make a living at small-scale agriculture and they are forced from the land. Some of the migration is due to the *pull* of the jobs in industry that the cities offer (Apichat et al. 1995). Often the appealing jobs in the cities don't exist, and migrants are forced into dark, dirty ghettos (Bangkok has over 1,000 slums with at least 800,000 inhabitants) and casual work with wages so low and conditions so dangerous that the migrants would clearly be better off back in the countryside (Akin 1993).

Accompanying the great social transformation of industrialization and the disruptions it causes, there are usually increases in all kinds of deviance, especially crime. And if all this is not too much for any society, these changes usually stimulate surges in population growth, which can be so massive that the standard of living for the majority of people drops as the demand from all of the new, unproductive mouths to feed greatly outstrips what the economy can provide.

The grim picture presented above, we must remind you, is meant to describe the countries of Europe going through the process of industrialization 300 or so years ago, not a nation of starving people in Africa, Latin America, or Asia today. It was in the middle of all this disruption in Europe that sociology in fact was born. People were worried, and sociological giants such as Durkheim, Tonnies, and Marx were in the business of trying to figure out why it was happening, where it was all going, and what perhaps could be done about it.

But there is a major difference for developing countries today. As we have seen in our chapter on the Thai economy, the effects of the **modern world system** have certainly made things more complex and difficult for many developing countries today compared to the European experience a few hundred years ago. Quite simply, there are two factors that differentiate the present development process from the past. First, there are now nations far ahead in the economic development race, and second, the pace of change is much more rapid. The advanced nations provide models to the less developed, which speeds up the development process, but they also provide powerful economic competition. So, for Western nations the transformation from agricultural societies to advanced industrialized nations took centuries, and the social strains and conflicts generated were worked out gradually; in today's developing countries, like Thailand, comparable transformations have occurred in just decades. In the worst case scenario, one experienced by some developing countries, the process of industrialization with all of the accompanying disruptions and dislocations is begun, only to prematurely terminate. The affected country remains stuck, unable to advance to the next stages of development where the problems are resolved through increasing wealth and the political and social institutions adapt to the changes in society. And it is already too late for the country affected to return to an earlier time of stable traditions. These countries, it is likely, would have been better off had they not started the process of development at all rather than to have begun and then gotten stuck.

In the case of Thailand, many of the social problems we will consider below are related to the disruptions associated with social change brought on by the process of industrialization. Writing at the end of the 20th century, there is reason for both optimism and caution regarding Thailand's prospects. It seems that Thailand will not get stuck and that its most serious social problems will abate at least to some degree as time goes on. On the other hand, no country, developed or developing, is without social problems, and those Thailand is experiencing at present are the result of both processes of economic development and the intrinsic failures and weaknesses of Thai society.

In what follows we will consider the major social problems affecting Thailand, many of which are typical of those facing a rapidly developing country as described above. One, a nonproblem for Thailand when compared to most other countries, race and ethnic conflict, has already been considered in our chapter on social stratification. And we can begin with what is another comparatively nonproblem in Thailand, population growth.

POPULATION PROBLEMS

As noted briefly in our introduction, one of the problems plaguing many, if not most, developing nations is rapid population growth. In what demographers call the **demographic transition,** the initial impact of economic development in a less developed country is a decrease in the death rate (mortality) due to improved health care, better nutrition, and more sanitary conditions, without an accompanying drop in what is usually a very high birth rate. Typically, in less developed societies where infant and child mortality rates are very high there is an economic rationale for having many children as they provide the necessary labor for the household unit of production and social security for parents in old age. Culture and religion play a role as they are in sync with the economic rationale and support the practice of having many children. With the onset of economic development, the combination of a declining death rate with a high and stable birth rate produces very rapid population growth.

What is rather unique for Thailand is that not only is rapid population growth not a problem, in fact, just the opposite is the case. As recently as the 1960s, Thailand did fit the demographic transition model and had a problem with too much population growth. But that was before the now-famous Thai senator Mechai began pushing the government to get involved by educating families and supplying birth control (Kulick and Wilson 1996: 2, 126). In 1970, Thailand still had a population growth rate of 3 percent a year; according to estimates by researchers at Mahidol University, Thailand now has a below-zero population growth, which is to say the Thai people overdid birth control and there are not enough children being produced to keep the population from shrinking (*The Nation,* July 16, 1996; *Bangkok Post,* July 22, 1996). Much of the research was focused on northern Thailand where there was an average of 5.2 children per family in 1960, which was down to 2.3 by 1980 (about the replacement rate), and finally down to 1.46 by 1990. In no other country in the world has the population growth rate dropped as quickly as in Thailand.

To a large degree, of course, this is a positive factor for Thailand. Fewer nonproductive children has helped rapidly raise the standard of living for Thais as the economy grew in the 1980s. But there are major drawbacks from low or zero population growth. For example, in 40 years Thailand will have over 25 percent of the population at 65 years old or older, compared to 3.6 percent at present. As it has in Japan and most of Europe, this situation will create a serious problem of caring for the aged, meaning much more spent on health care and social security, with a much higher tax rate on the small percentage of the population at working age to pay for it (*International Herald Tribune,* July 11, 1998). Other negative effects are a worsening labor shortage, which Thailand has had for a number of years; in addition, recently 10 percent of the elementary schools were closed. Once a nation such as Thailand has been so successful in changing attitudes supporting large families, it is rather doubtful these attitudes will again change, suggesting that Thailand's success in reducing population growth is unlikely to be met with a successful program to increase it again.

PROSTITUTION

It is time to turn to what is certainly not a nonproblem in Thailand; rather, it is one of the worst problems: prostitution, which is significantly related to another of the major problems we will discuss below, AIDS. Currently prostitution is illegal, but the operation of a facility where prostitution occurs is not. Prostitution is more than tolerated, it is condoned and encouraged in official circles. The owners of places of prostitution, sometimes high-level government officials, are technically committing no crime, while the prostitutes themselves are.

Since prostitution is technically illegal, the actual number of commercial sex workers is almost impossible to estimate. Most of the women in this occupation are between 15 and 29 years old; the average length of time working in the sex industry is 18 months to two years, and in any given year there is considerable turnover. Some women may also work as sex workers on a seasonal basis. The most accurate estimate is probably between 200–300 thousand women working as prostitutes within a given year (8 to 9 percent of the women in the age range). From a broader perspective, a conservative estimate places at least as many as 1.2 million people in some degree economically dependent on the sex industry (Wathinee and Guest 1994: 29–38). There are estimates of as many as 100,000 male prostitutes as well, providing services primarily to male clients but also to women.

In 1994, the organization End Child Prostitution in Asian Tourism (ECPAT) received the 1993 Anti-Slavery Award given annually by Anti-Slavery International, the oldest anti-slavery organization in the world. News coverage about the award has described the extent of child prostitution in Thailand and ECPAT's efforts to combat it, as would be expected. Moreover, the coverage has reported that Thailand's huge sex-for-sale industry is driven primarily by European and American tourists (Ehrlich 1994). Much of the media coverage of prostitution in Thailand does contain some statements of fact—child prostitution and actual sex slavery are major problems, and there is a huge sex industry as described above. Where much of the media coverage diverges from accuracy, however, is when the primary cause for this sex industry is identified as the clientele of Western and Japanese tourists. Sex tourism is certainly big in Thailand, and one estimate is that, unique for any country in the world, about 50 percent of tourists to Thailand in recent years have been unaccompanied males (Shearer 1989: 73). But there is much more to explain the existence of a large and comprehensive sex industry in Thailand, as virtually every town, including those seldom frequented by foreigners, has at least one facility offering prostitution. And again, while difficult to estimate accurately, one study found that three-fourths of married Thai men engaged in extramarital sex, including visiting prostitutes (Napaporn, Bennett, and Knodel 1993)

A number of studies done by Thai scholars identify prostitution as existing from the time of the early Ayudhya period 500 to 600 years ago (Skrobanek 1987), and an account of an early French visitor in 1687 noted that sexually transmitted diseases were common (Bamber, Hewison, and Underwood 1994). In 1909, the government required the licensing of prostitutes to control venereal disease; and in the late 1920s, over 700 were licensed in Bangkok alone. Thai literature going back many decades also describes prostitution; in fact, one famous book written in the 1920s called *The Prostitute* details a system of prostitution quite similar to that found today in Thailand, complete with descriptions of peasant girls tricked into the sex trade.

Any explanation for extensive prostitution in Thailand must note that Thais have viewed sex rather casually throughout history. As someone put it, they simply missed the puritan age of the Europeans. Only recently have middle- and upper-middle-class parents been socializing their daughters into a more puritanical value system, which is much influenced by the assimilation of Chinese and middle-class Western values in the Thai cities today. And we should again note that any explanation of the status and behavior of women in Thai society today must recognize many complexities and contradictions due to the combinations of cultures in the 20th century. There is no other way to explain the quite inhibited behavior of most female college students on the Chulalongkorn University campus (where the big issue in 1998 was prohibiting skirt lengths above the knee), while the campus is within easy walking distance from perhaps the biggest and most famous red-light district in the world.

Offering historical and cultural explanations for prostitution, many scholars suggest a link to the social system established in Ayudhya whereby men were required to spend months each year away from their families. A more complex cultural interpretation, however, involves the effects of the collision of two cultures, that of the northern matrilocal culture of old Thailand and the patrilineal culture in the south.[7]

As described earlier, when compared to the rest of the world, and especially Asia, Thailand is somewhat unique in the extent to which a matrilocal family system has existed in some parts of the country, particularly in the north. A matrilocal family system, in which females retain the family farmland and husbands are required to move in with the wife's parents, not only gives females more freedom, it also confers upon them great responsibility to help provide for the extended family (Akin 1993; Muecke 1992). If there is not sufficient means of support on the farm, then girls have the responsibility of leaving for the city or other

areas where work might be found. The collision of this culture with a
patrilineal male-dominant family system not far away, with males who
are taught that the pursuit and exploitation of women is acceptable or
even required to show real manhood, has resulted in a well-established
system of prostitution. There are women ready to provide sex for sale,
and who can return home with respect because of the money they bring
to support their family, and there are men who need to pursue women as
sex objects to gain status among their male peers.

Today, many of the young women from northern Thailand continue to return home without loss of respect and are even admired for
showing filial piety in taking care of their parents by sending home
money, despite their work as prostitutes (Shearer 1989: 70; Mulder 1994:
54–55). And send money they do: One estimate in 1979 was that the post
office in a little northern town of Dok Kham Thai transferred some
$1.7 million from girls working in Bangkok (Shearer 1989: 165). In some
instances prostitution has actually altered the normal preference of families for male children; in some villages in the north, the birth of a daughter is celebrated with the view that god has given the parents a valuable
commodity (Akin 1993). On the other hand, most families and the larger
village community, especially in the northeast, feel shame that their
daughters are involved in prostitution, and there is a stigma[8] attached to
being a prostitute (Pasuk 1982).

Other explanations for the large sex industry in Thailand today focus
on two aspects of the country's economic development. In the process of
economic development certain sectors of society have been marginalized,
become relatively poorer as the society as a whole has become richer. The
most marginalized in Thai society are rural women, especially the young
women in the northeast and the north, who are among the least educated
in these two poorest regions of the country. They are the victims of trends
seen in many developing nations where, despite rapid industrialization,
the industrial sector of the economy has not absorbed all the available
labor, demand for labor in agriculture has decreased with mechanization,
and the service economy, of which prostitution is a part, has dispropor-
tionately absorbed surplus labor (see Table 3–1). With poverty, the loss of
secondary sources of nonfarm income from forests around villages, and
unemployment in the provinces, there are strong financial incentives for
some women to choose prostitution (Pasuk 1982),[9] and as we have noted
above, the old matrilocal cultures in these areas reinforce this choice.
While this explanation emphasizes the supply side of prostitution, on the
demand side, economic development has lead to an increase in the spending power of men generally, especially the new middle class. Therefore,
more men are able to afford to pay for sexual services, and culture reinforces the desire of many men to do so.

The international dimension to prostitution is twofold, involving
sex tourism, whereby men come to Thailand seeking sex, and the
international trafficking in women. For instance, it is estimated that there

are perhaps 120,000 Thai women working in Japan illegally, of whom 80 percent are prostitutes. Thai government figures are considerably lower, estimating about 25,000 (*Bangkok Post*, August 19, 1996). During the 1980s, about 90 percent of these women were tricked into the trade, though this had fallen to 60 percent in the 1990s as more women entered voluntarily. The traffic in women is well organized (*Bangkok Post*, May 17, 1998). Some are recruited directly from rural villages with the promise of high-paying jobs in other industries. But once they are in the country of destination they are informed of the large debt they owe for being transported and smuggled and then forced to pay it back through prostitution. Women who pay off the debt can make as much as 6,000 to 9,000 dollars a month in countries such as Japan.

As do the owners of the establishments of prostitution, the agents and traffickers make much more of the total profit than do the sex workers (*Bangkok Post*, August 19, 1996). Although Japan and Malaysia are the most well researched destinations, Thai women are also trafficked to Taiwan and other Asian countries, to Europe (where there are an estimated 10,000 Thai prostitutes), and to North America. Women are also trafficked from neighboring countries into prostitution, either in Thailand or some other destination, especially from Burma, Cambodia, Laos, and southern China. Although exact numbers are not available, there may be as many as 40,000 women from Burma working as prostitutes in Thailand.

Just as children are part of the labor force generally, child prostitution is a part of the sex industry in Thailand. And as with adult prostitutes, estimates of the number of children working in prostitution vary greatly. High estimates provided by the Center for the Protection of Children's Rights place the number at 800,000, while the Ministry of Public Health in Thailand estimates 15,000. Academic estimates put the figure at 30–40,000. Certainly the extreme high and low estimates are wrong, but at least 30,000 and as many as 100,000 children may work as child prostitutes in Thailand (Guest 1994; Orachai and Chanya 1994).

Besides the economic, social, and cultural factors associated with prostitution generally, child prostitution is driven by additional factors. Some men, mistakenly, believe they are much less likely to contract the AIDS virus if they patronize child prostitutes. Some Asian men believe that having sex with a very young woman brings luck; and some older men believe it can invigorate them. Of course pedophile demand for sex with child prostitutes is also a factor.

Some of these young girls are in effect sent into prostitution by their families, either to pay off debts incurred by the parents or to generate family income. Most, however, are tricked and coerced into the industry with offers of legitimate jobs after which they are forced into prostitution when removed from the family's protection. Thai people have been just as shocked and outraged as the rest of the world when recent stories emerged of parents in northern Thailand selling their daughters into prostitution to support the parents' drug use.

AIDS

It is fitting to follow our description of prostitution in Thailand with two related subjects, one is a result and the other is another aspect of the cause. One result, of course, is AIDS, and another aspect of the cause of prostitution is a wider problem of corruption in the Thai society. This subject will be considered later.

Thailand's AIDS epidemic, at least before the late 1990s, may have been the most severe in the world, more severe than in sub–Saharan Africa, in scope and impact. Cases of AIDS were reported in Thailand as early as 1984, first with intravenous drug users, then commercial sex workers and young heterosexual men. Among men with sexually transmitted diseases, the rate of AIDS infection was zero in 1989, but it was 6 percent by 1992. In northern Thailand the rate of infection among female brothel workers has been consistently found to be 40 percent or higher (Mastro et al. 1994). The rate in the general population is probably best represented by the numbers in Table 8–1 below. It demonstrates the continuing increase of the spread of the disease among the female population, most of whom are not prostitutes, as they become infected by their partners. The rapid increase from 1989 until 1993, and the subsequent decrease, among the young male military conscripts reflects the onset of the epidemic and the impact of the AIDS prevention campaign described below. Mechai Viravaidhya, a senator and the president of the Population and Community Development Association, has called HIV/AIDS a national disaster. This organization estimates that Thailand has 850,000 HIV-positive cases and 60,000 people with full-blown AIDS. In 1996 there were 10,000 AIDS orphans in Thailand, and it is estimated that by the year 2000 there will be as many as 120,000 (*Bangkok Post,* August 13, 1996). More than 20,000 HIV-positive women give birth in Thailand each year (*Bangkok Post,* September 24, 1996).

TABLE 8–1

Rates of Female and Male HIV Infection Illustrated by Percentage of Pregnant Women and Male Military Conscripts Testing Positive, 1989–1995.

	1989	1990	1991	1992	1993	1994	1995
Pregnant women	0.00%	0.00%	0.80%	1.00%	1.39%	1.78%	2.29%
Male conscripts	0.00	1.60	2.90	3.60	3.96	3.40	2.50

Sources: For *pregnant women:* Division of Epidemiology, Public Health Ministry. For *male military conscripts:* Army Institute of Pathology, Royal Thai Army (presented in *Bangkok Post* June 30, 1996: 22)

The news, however, is not all bad in contrast to what is typically reported in the Western media about Thailand. Successful action is being taken.

Both authors happened upon one of the beginning campaigns of this action to reduce AIDS in Thailand during 1990. After leaving a restaurant in Bangkok we heard noises from a large crowd of people in a nearby street. Being social scientists, an investigation was mandatory. What we found was a Miss Anti-AIDS pageant in the middle of one of the red-light districts of Bangkok. In the street was a stage where several girls from the bars/brothels were receiving votes from the crowd for the title of Miss Anti-AIDS. In the process of it all, however, was the real goal of the program: Hundreds of little cards about AIDS, its causes and prevention, were being distributed, along with thousands of packets of condoms. At the end of the crowning ceremony a man dressed in what can best be described as a Superman costume jumped on stage to throw more cards about AIDS and condoms to the crowd, and then the whole procession moved into each of the bars, one at a time, to repeat the process on stages where the bar girls dance and draw the attention of potential customers. We had happened upon one of Senator Mechai's programs. After pushing for the highly successful program to reduce population growth noted above, Senator Mechai has now taken up the cause of reducing AIDS.

At the 11th International Conference on AIDS sponsored by the United Nations, research data were announced showing that Thailand and only one other country in the world have had a similar large drop in HIV-positive cases (*Bangkok Post,* July 10, 1996). Thailand was called a model for success in preventing AIDS. There has been an 80 percent drop in all sexually transmitted diseases in Thailand since 1984, and the number of new infections each year has dropped almost fourfold since 1990. All of the Thai measures, it was estimated, have probably led to preventing about 2 million future cases of HIV.

Once the government began a policy drive to control the spread of AIDS, it concentrated on promoting condom use and public awareness campaigns rather than attempting the rather impossible task of stopping prostitution in Thailand. It is even reported that Senator Mechai sponsored a program whereby prostitutes measured their clients to make sure the standard condom fit properly and was effective (Kulick and Wilson 1996: 126). The Population and Research Institute at Mahidol University estimates that condom use increased 75 percent from 1990 to 1994. According to studies of army draftees in six northern provinces, the rate of infection decreased from 13 percent in 1991 to 7 percent in 1995. And condom use by the men in encounters with prostitutes had risen from 61 percent to 93 percent in the same period (*Bangkok Post,* June 30, 1996). And equally important to all of this, Thailand had the largest government budget of any developing country in its AIDS control program.

None of this is to say that Thailand has no AIDS problem. Even with the improvements the problem is serious, causing great human suffering and a drop in the Thai standard of living due to the medical costs borne by the state and the loss of productivity in the economy. However, Thailand has shown other developing countries that rational action can be taken to effectively do something about a problem that is affecting much of the world.

CORRUPTION

According to the Political Economy Research Centre at Chulalongkorn University the "black," or illegal, economy in Thailand comprises six major businesses: drugs, smuggling, gambling, arms dealing, illegal migrant labor, and the sex industry. This illegal economy is so large, generating revenue equivalent to 15–18 percent of the country's gross national product annually, that it poses a threat to the long-term economic stability of the country. The two most profitable sectors are gambling and prostitution (*Bangkok Post*, November 25, 1996). The researchers pointed out the obvious: that this level of corruption could not exist without the cooperation and participation of many high-level bureaucrats, politicians, and the police.

The reaction to the research, especially the charge of payoffs to police to protect illegal casinos, demonstrated this point. Citing humiliation and loss of dignity and reputation, 16 police station chiefs in Bangkok who were indirectly accused of complicity in casino gambling filed defamation complaints against the researchers. Police were sent to "observe" the researchers' homes and activities, a clear and not uncommon act of intimidation, and the author of the offending paper received a bomb threat. The deputy commissioner of the Central Investigation Bureau of the police department had attended the seminar at which the research was presented. Quite reasonably, he had admitted the validity of the allegations of official complicity in the obvious illegal gambling that was occurring. He, in turn, became the subject of an investigation (*Bangkok Post*, November 25, 1996). NGOs, labor leaders, and social and political activists rallied to defend the researcher; university officials and higher-ranking police generals met, with the prime minister as mediator, to discuss the situation, and eventually the controversy died away (see various issues of the *Bangkok Post* from July 26, to August 12, 1996). The incident well illustrates the two most important points regarding corruption in Thailand: the scope of corruption is immense, and official complicity at very high levels of government is the order of the day. While the controversy caused by the research soon died away (as is usually the case in Thailand), what did not change is the reality of corruption in Thai society. Although we cannot cover all the complexities and nuances of corruption in Thailand, we can provide an overview of the syndrome by explaining some of its historical development and then look at current practice in one significant institution, the national police force.

The historical source of such high levels of corruption is thought to be found in the **gin muang** system of administration practiced during the Ayudhyan and early Bangkok periods, as described in Chapter 2 (Keyes 1989). Under this system, governmental administration was sub-contracted out to individuals who received no salaries for their services. The individuals holding administrative offices were expected to provide the monarchy its due as per the contract and obtain for themselves what they could above this amount. In this system, obtaining a position in government became a means of accumulating wealth rather than serving the public. The practice of accumulating wealth was reinforced by the common view that going into royal service was a form of personal sacri-fice and that it was therefore appropriate for this sacrifice to be repaid in the form of gifts from the citizens overseen by officials. In Thai this is known as the gin muang system, which means "to eat the state" (Pasuk and Songsidh 1996: 110). When King Chulalongkorn established a mod-ern salaried professional bureaucracy through his reforms late in the 19th century, the practice of gin muang and the expectation of many offi-cials that their positions entitled them to gifts and other forms of addi-tional income persisted. The practice remains at the heart of much of the corruption throughout the bureaucracy (Pasuk and Sungsidh 1996). At the lowest level, the practice of giving any government official a small sum for the performance of a duty—the giving of "tea money"—is ac-ceptable. Of course, it is but a small step from tea money to extortion, and from there to what amounts to looting the national government.

THE POLICE

Recently, one of the authors observed an American professor presenting a lecture on American culture to a class of mature Thai graduate stu-dents, many of whom were parents. It was really an excellent lecture, with pictures from *Life* magazine used to illustrate the main points. Dis-playing a slide of a policeman talking to a young boy at what appeared to be an amusement park, the professor explained how American chil-dren are taught to contact friendly and helpful policemen if they were lost or in trouble; the professor innocently stated, "I suppose you do the same thing in Thailand." Her statement was followed by an exceedingly awkward moment of uncomprehending and embarrassed silence on the part of the student audience. Pressed to respond, eventually a few of the students broke the silence by saying no, that is not what Thai children are taught, in fact, they are taught to avoid the police at all costs. As we shall see in the description of the Thai police force, there is good reason Thai children are socialized much differently with regard to trusting the police than are American children.

The national police provide a useful case study of the pervasiveness of corruption. In a national study, the highest percentage of the respondents, 33 percent, viewed the police as the most corrupt government department[10] (Pasuk and Songsidh 1996: 156). The national police force was created during King Chulalongkorn's reforms, and like the rest of the bureaucracy it is a centralized national government agency. There are no subsidiary police forces at the provincial or lower levels of administration. From its inception the primary function of the police has been some form of national security, first in support of the monarchy, then military government, later anti-communism, but never has its purpose been to serve and protect the community. In fact, the police are accountable only to their superiors within the bureaucracy and ultimately the Minister of Interior.

The tendency to corruption inherited through the gin muang system is reinforced by the consistently low salaries payed to all officials, including the police; and it is generally accepted that a position in the police force entitles the official to some additional personal income through corruption. Individual police units are also expected to raise some of their own funds, such as for improving police stations and purchasing equipment, through the gin muang system. The extra income derived from the higher positions on the police force is great; thus, just as money plays a significant role in the election process and in obtaining positions in parliament and the cabinet, large sums are paid to superiors within the police department to obtain promotions. There is a three-part police code of honor amounting to a code of silence: Don't bring down your brothers, don't tell on your bosses, don't betray your friends (*Bangkok Post*, December 13, 1996). Police corruption ranges from the large-scale, fully organized type, such as police alliances with gangster syndicates (gambling, prostitution), to the petty harassment of the poor and working class in the form of extortion. Often it is even necessary to offer a gift to the police to have a crime such as house burglary investigated.

Once, riding down to Pattaya from Bangkok, we were motioned to pull over by a traffic policeman. The driver disgustedly got out of the car promising to return in a minute. Upon our friend's return we asked what the stop was all about, and he disgustedly replied "lunch money." The policeman was hungry and basically extorted his lunch out of a convenient driver. Similarly, truck drivers are required to pay unofficial tolls to police as they travel the highways from one district to the next; and in a great example of gin muang, a recent scandal involved the traffic police in Bangkok giving undeserved citations for violations of vehicle emission standards to the tune of millions of baht, of which the police kept 70 percent. Similar forms of corruption range from those in which citizens need to pay government officials for the performance of their official duties, to bribes for special favors and consideration, to highly organized multimillion dollar scams. All types permeate much of the government bureaucracy. The high levels of corruption erode public confidence in the government and constitute perhaps the single greatest obstacle to the solution of pressing social problems like those presented in this chapter.

POLITICAL VIOLENCE

We can define **political violence** as violence that has the goal of promoting or preventing social change in a society. Such political violence can be used by revolutionaries trying to make change, as well as the more typical case of governments using violence to keep others from producing change. As a result of the disruptions and social problems produced by economic development, countries going through this process often experience political violence. The sectors of society most harmed in the development process, even if temporarily, often decide to pick up guns to force the government to institute policy that can reduce their suffering, or they even attempt to change the nature of the political system and those in charge. Further, many developing countries today suffer from the legacies of colonialism. European powers created national boundaries for their new colonies based on a purely economic rationale of controlling resources and markets for exploitation; and in agreements with the other colonial powers, they divided up the spoils to prevent conflict. Thus, as is especially the case in Africa, tribal and ethnic divisions among people who have been at war for centuries were ignored, and these hostile groups were forced to coexist in the same nation. When these countries became independent after World War II, years of internal warfare resulted.

As we have noted many times, for the most part Thailand has been free of destabilizing political violence. There has been nothing in Thai history, for example, like the massive political violence carried out in Indonesia to the south in 1965 and 1998, with perhaps a million people killed in 1965. There have been mass protests against the military's involvement in politics, especially in the mid-1970s, and then briefly for the last time in 1991. From the 1960s into the 1980s there was a rural-based communist insurgency in Thailand; but while there was considerable violence, it never achieved the levels found in Vietnam, Cambodia, and Laos. After the violent reinstitution of military government in 1976, some young people took to the jungles to join this rebellion, but for most their participation was short-lived and the commitment to socialism rather weak. In recent years, however, the only political violence to speak of in Thailand has been carried out by separatist rebels in the south.

As noted earlier, the four most southern provinces of Thailand have populations that are 80 percent Muslim and historically more related to the people and culture of Malaysia than to Thailand. At the end of World War II, when the former British colony became free, the new Malaysian boundaries did not include these four provinces, which remain with Thailand. From the beginning there was discontent among these Islamic Thais who felt neglected and exploited by the Thai government. By the mid-1980s there was formation of the Gerakan Mujahidin Islam Pattani (GMIP) and later the Pattani United Liberation Organization. (See several articles in the *Bangkok Post* during late 1997 and early 1998, but especially January 18, 1998, summarizing the history of these separatist groups.)

The political violence by the GMIP and PULO have been concentrated on symbols of the Thai government in the area, such as schools and teachers, the police, public buildings, and the railroad system. A few people have been killed. But as of the spring of 1998, most of the main leaders of these separatist movements have been arrested after a new wave of political violence. The Malaysian government then began cooperating with Thailand in locating these leaders hiding across the border in Malaysia. While never attracting a large following, these separatists were successful and bring more attention to the plight of southern Muslims in Thailand. A result of this has been development projects, some sponsored by the king himself, that have improved economic conditions for people in the area.

THE ENVIRONMENT

It is unfortunately common for developing countries to pay little attention to their environments, with a race to produce more economic growth usually polluting their rivers and air and destroying their forests. This behavior is understandable, which is not to say acceptable, when we consider that these societies are focused on reducing poverty and creating employment as quickly as possible for their citizens (not to mention more wealth for the wealthy). We could even suggest our own "theory of trash," which maintains that there is a correlation between the level of economic development in the country and the amount of trash in the streets, forests, and rivers. Certainly there are cultural influences as well, but people who are still poor and worried about putting food on the table generally have less time and energy left over to worry about the trash. It is only as a country becomes more developed economically that people start giving more attention to the trash.

Much the same can be said about pollution and the environment, and unfortunately Thailand is among the worst offenders (Muscat 1994: 235). Bangkok is a city from the developed world in terms of industry and consumption without the legal and environmental protections found in a developed nation. According to the World Health Organization, unrestrained development has been making Bangkok one of the most polluted cities in the world (*Bangkok Post*, November 13, 1997). Traffic congestion is a major problem, costing the country more than three billion dollars annually. While new roads are increasing at a rate of 1.5 percent annually, the number of cars is increasing by 10 percent[11] (Balch 1996). With the congestion, travel that took 30 minutes 20 years ago often takes two hours or more today; many commuters spend four hours or more on a daily commute, and cars stand idle and pump out pollutants. During rush hour in some extremely congested areas, levels of lead in the air reach ten times the average level found in U.S. urban areas.

The structural change in the Thai economy, with rapid growth of the industrialized sector, along with the concentration of manufacturing in the Bangkok area, have generated environmental problems with which the country is ill prepared to cope. All kinds of trash and chemicals have been dumped into the central river (Chao Phaya) running through Thailand and the city of Bangkok, leading some researchers to suggest nothing may live in the river in a few decades (Kulick and Wilson 1996: 121). The city of Bangkok, it is also suggested, may some day become unlivable (Pasuk and Baker 1996b: 237). As an indication of the rapid change, in 1979 industries producing hazardous waste accounted for 29 percent of the kingdom's GDP; by 1989 the proportion was 58 percent. In 1986, Thai industries produced 1.1 million tons of hazardous waste, a figure expected to rise to about 5.7 million tons in 2010, and industrial pollutants are increasing at an exponential rate of 12–15 percent per year.

Concentration in Bangkok and rapid growth mean that the waste cannot be assimilated by the environment. While environmental awareness (see below) has developed and legislation has been passed, enforcement remains extremely weak. If Thailand does not develop an effective policy of pollution control in the near future it stands to become a **pollution haven** for highly polluting industries not accepted in more developed countries (Panayotu, Phanu, and Krerkpong 1994). In fact, Thailand may already have followed this path since industries established through foreign investment account for a majority of the hazardous waste.

The impact of development has been equally dramatic in the rural sector. The agricultural expansion that fueled development was accomplished through the expansion of the amount of land under cultivation, with the result that only about 30 percent of Thailand's hardwood forests remain and much of that is quite degraded. In general, forests are important for their contribution to biological diversity, watershed protection, and prevention of soil erosion, not to mention reduction in greenhouse gases and the slowdown of potential global warming. In a developing country like Thailand, forests are much more important than their contribution to GDP or the environmental factors above might indicate. Forests remain a significant source of food for many villagers, and according to some estimates, the amount of wood used for fuel in an informal manner far exceeds the total contribution of forest products to GDP—both of these usages constitute an important type of informal income to the poor rural sector of society. If further forest depletion occurs they will have to purchase food and fuel in the market economy (Sadoff 1994).

Things, however, are changing in Thailand. There is finally some success in reducing traffic congestion in Bangkok, with many new roads now in place; but better yet, to keep out more cars rather than just making more room for them, a new elevated train system was completed in 1999, and a subway system is in the advanced planning stage. For the country as a whole, however, most important has been one of the most active environmental protest movements in the world (Pasuk and Baker 1996a: 148–58). Farmers, students, and citizens of all kinds have been marching in the streets, blocking dams and pipe lines, monitoring forests to prevent illegal logging, and even bringing court action against hill tribe people who continue their old methods of "slash and burn" agriculture in northern Thailand.

There have been improvements in the quality of the Thai environment because of these actions, but there are still questions about whether the destruction of the environment has gone on so long that many areas will not be cleaned up for decades and forests will never be restored.

CONCLUSION

It seems fitting that we end this book with a picture of the good and bad of Thailand today. Thailand has much to be proud of when looking back over recent decades. Compared to other developing nations around the world, Thailand can be proud of its rather steady economic development, which has dramatically reduced poverty in the last two decades of the 20th century. Yes, income inequality did increase significantly with the economic bubble of the late 1980s and up to 1997. But as 1999 draws to a close, there is evidence that the economy is starting to move forward again, and with less of the uneven development experienced with the "golf course capitalism" of the economic bubble years.

Compared to other developing nations and especially those around it in Southeast Asia today, perhaps Thailand can be most proud of its political democracy. We must be clear that democracy is a relative term; countries can be rated on degrees of democracy. But while there are many blocks to pure popular democracy in Thailand today, there has been improvement in recent years. And compared to other Southeast Asian nations, Thailand is a virtual oasis of democracy.

Having said all of the above, however, we have spent considerable time in this last chapter showing how Thailand still has a long way to go in overcoming many kinds of social problems that commonly plague developing countries. Particularly troubling are the problems of child prostitution and AIDS in Thailand, though as we have shown, some improvements have been made. But corruption, destruction of the environment, and other social problems have shown little or no improvement in recent years. As Thailand emerges from the economic crisis of the late 1990s and moves into the 21st century, we should watch closely to see if the Thai foundation of comparatively strong economic, political, and family institutions will help the country reduce these other social problems, making it a model for many other developing nations in the world.

END NOTES

1. With respect to the extensive use of first names primarily among Thai people it is important to note as well that we have followed the Thai tradition when citing works by Thai authors. References and citations in this book will list the Thai first name of the author, and this first name will govern the alphabetical order of Thai authors in the reference list.

2. It is this value orientation of "radical individualism" that is increasingly cited as partially responsible for many of our social problems—from the highest divorce rate and rate of single-parent families among industrial nations, to the high crime rates and low educational success compared to other nations. See especially, Bellah et al. (1985) and Etzioni (1984).

3. For more detailed explanation of this type of historical and comparative research and the effects of the material environment, see Gouldner and Peterson (1962), Heise, Lenski, and Wardwell (1976), Lenski (1966, 1978), and Lenski and Nolan (1986).

4. For example, Bollen and Appold (1993) have found the relationship between corporate involvement in poor nations and less economic development over the long term to be affected by such things as the *type* of goods imported or exported. Also, Lenski and Nolan (1984, 1986) have found that the level of technology within the poor nation at the time it is brought into the world system is important in influencing whether or not the poor nation can achieve economic growth. Developing nations that have more advanced agriculture when brought into the world system through core investments are more likely to have some economic growth.

5. Of course, it is often argued that America students score lower because we send a greater percentage of our young people on to high schools compared to countries such as Thailand, which only have their brightest and most motivated in high schools. But even when we compare only the top 5 percent of American high school seniors to the top 5 percent in these other countries, the American students still score below average.

6. Here and elsewhere information is based upon several personal interviews with a number of officials in the Thai Ministry of Education between 1994 and 1998.

7. This is based upon interviews with anthropologists at the University of Chiang Mai and Hill Tribe Research Institute in Chiang Mai, Thailand. To our knowledge this theoretical explanation of early Thai prostitution has not been published in English.

8. But many young women know the Thai saying "money will shut their mouths" regarding those who look down on them for having been prostitutes. It should also be noted that in this, as in many other instances, Buddhism is essentially nonjudgmental, instead seeing the actions as a result of, as well as contributing to, one's kamma.

9. One study found that in Thailand these marginalized young women can make 25 times more as prostitutes than in any other job (*Los Angeles Times,* January 26, 1996, p. A5). In 1980 it was estimated that a prostitute in Bangkok could make about $400 per month, compared to a waitress or factory worker making about $32 per month, or a clerical worker making $52 per month (Shearer 1989: 66).

10. The rest, in order, are as follows: the Ministry of Defense (27%), Ministry of Interior (26%), Department of Transport (22.5%), and the Land Department (10.1%). According to the study, the public did not differentiate between military and civilian governments in terms of levels of corruption. The single largest group of respondents consisted of those who couldn't say which was more corrupt (34.2%), while 23 percent chose military government and 22.2 percent chose civilian (Pasuk and Songsidh 1996: 156–57) More recently, the Ministries of Education and Commerce have come to been seen as excessively corrupt (*Bangkok Post,* July 2, 1998).

11. An interesting example that illustrates the traffic problem is the following. In 1994 it would have required 6,000 kilometers of two-lane roads filled bumper to bumper to hold all the cars registered in Bangkok, but there were less than 3,000 kilometers of roads in the metropolitan area.

GLOSSARY

animism   The traditional belief system in Southeast Asia that spirits inhabit every existing thing, including objects, places, and processes in nature. The spirit world is separate but intertwined with the natural world.

anthropocentric   Used with reference to Buddhism, which interprets the world from the human perspective with emphasis on human values and experiences as opposed to emphasis on the supernatural.

Ayudhya   The name of the second old capital of Thailand that existed from 1350 to 1767; also describes this period in Thai history.

Buddhism   Buddhism is an individualistic religious and philosophical tradition that originated with the historical Buddha (c. 563–483 B.C.) in India; it holds that suffering is inherent in life and that one can escape it into nirvana by mental and moral self-purification.

bunkhun   A psychological bond between two people based on gratefulness for favors given and the willingness to reciprocate by giving favors in return. The strongest such relationship is that between parents and children, especially daughters toward their parents. Bunkhun relationships permeate Thai life.

capitalist development state   A capitalist industrialist economy wherein the state has extensive control in managing the economy with major policies oriented toward economic development.

caste system   A system of social stratification based upon status rankings and strict ascription. This caste system was found in its most complete sense in pre-colonized India, but many elements of a caste system were instituted in Thailand with the sakdina system.

class   In one of the most general definitions it is a grouping of individuals with similar positions and similar political and economic interests within the stratification system. According to Max Weber, it is a dimension of social stratification based upon property ownership or the lack of ownership (as in Marxian theory) but also occupational skill level.

collectivist value system   A value system emphasizing that the group is more important than the individual and individual desires, requiring greater sacrifice for group interests.

corporate class   A socioeconomic class within the society made up of the top corporate managers and their families who control the major corporations; in contrast to an upper class, such families do not primarily own these corporations.

corvee   Obligatory unpaid labor for public works as a substitute for taxes. This mandatory yearly labor of six to three months was characteristic of Thailand from early Ayudhya until abolished in 1905.

coup (coup d'etat)   The action of a group to seize or solidify control of a government through sudden illegal action. Distinguished from a revolution in that coup plotters have no intention of instituting wide-ranging social and economic change but wish to have the benefits of political leadership for themselves.

culture   The values and behaviors of a group that distinguish it from other groups.

culture shock   The disorientation that can occur when an individual moves from a familiar culture into one much different. The thoughts and behaviors that defined the culture to which the individual is accustomed do not work to achieve the same result in the new; the individual must rapidly learn those new behaviors.

demographic transition   A process through which most developing countries move from high birth rates and high death rates to stable population growth with low birth rates and low death rates.

dhamma (dharma)   In Buddhism, the truth that the Lord Buddha taught. The law, doctrine, duty, way of life in Buddhism.

ethnic group   A group of people relatively distinct in cultural background compared to the dominate group in the society.

export-oriented industrialization   An economic development strategy in which the government promotes the utilization of cheap labor to provide products for the world market, thereby stimulating economic growth.

extended family   A family that includes all relatives related by blood, marriage, or adoption (including father, mother, children, grandparents, close cousins, aunts, uncles) who compose a single household or live close to each other.

face   An individual's personal honor, dignity, and respect. Preserving face is very important in Thai culture. One can grasp its meaning somewhat from the phrase "saving face," meaning to prevent embarrassment.

family   The master institution in a society, with roles and norms associated with taking care of personal needs and caring for and socializing the young.

feudal-estate system (feudalism)   A hierarchical form of social, economic, and political organization with the king at the head, a chain of nobles below the king, and peasants at the bottom. The king or subordinate lords offer protection and sometimes land to the peasants in exchange for military and other services.

gender   Socially acquired and socially defined sex-linked behavior expectations in a particular society.

genocide   The planned and deliberate mass killing of a people based on their ethnic, racial, or national status.

gin muang   An expression that means "to eat the state," expressing the idea that government employees will use extra legal means to gain wealth.

green revolution   The practice of employing new agricultural technology, including new equipment, crop varieties, and chemicals, to dramatically increase crop yields. This practice, however, usually leads to greater inequality and uneven economic development because agricultural workers lose jobs due to the new technology while land owners become wealthy.

gross domestic product (GDP)   The total value of all goods and services produced within a nation in a given time period.

hierarchy   The ranking of individuals and groups in the society, a characteristic highly pronounced in the Thai society.

hill tribes   Groups of ethnic peoples in Thailand usually living in the northern mountain regions today. These groups have primarily kept to their old traditions of slash and burn agriculture and remain poor in modern Thailand.

ideal types   A method of categorizing social phenomena for simple comparison; this method can help us identify primary characteristics of social phenomena for more detailed analysis in the next stages of research.

import substitution industrialization   An industrialization strategy in which the government identifies imported goods that can be locally produced and then uses policy means to develop and protect new industrial enterprises producing these goods as a means to economic growth.

individualism (or individualistic value system)   Characterizes societies where the individuals are more important than groups.

individualistic value system   A value system emphasizing the greater importance of the individual and individual freedoms over group needs and restraints.

institutions   An abstract way of defining the problem-solving groupings in society. Family, the economy, religion, polity (the way formal power is organized), criminal justice, and so forth are all abstractions, referring to the way roles and norms are organized to deal with specific tasks faced by any society.

instrumental values   Social values related to modes of conduct. For any culture the socially defined appropriate means for achieving the goals defined by terminal values.

Islam   The religion founded by Muhammad during the seventh century in what is now Saudi Arabia. It is practiced most in the Middle East and is the predominant religion in parts of Southeast Asia, such as Malaysia, Indonesia, and southern Thailand.

jao-phor   A Thai rendering of the English word *godfather*, as in the movie about the mafia. It describes people with both legitimate and illegitimate business interests who can exercise a strong influence in politics.

kamma (karma)   The process of the accumulation of good or bad merit through intentional acts that result in states of being and rebirth during the process of reincarnation.

matriarchy   Refers to a society in which women are head of the family and descent and kinship are defined through the female line. More generally it refers to a society in which women are dominant.

matrilineal   A system of tracing descent through the female line and of inheriting property and family identity primarily through one's mother.

matrilocal residence   Describes the practice of a newly married couple living with the wife's parents.

modern world system   The system of unequal power and economic roles among nations similar to an international stratification system that has been closely linked with capitalism and colonialism developing since the 1500s.

multidimensional view of stratification   The perspective originated by Max Weber that argues that Marx's view of ownership versus nonownership of the means of production as the most important dimension of social stratification is too simple. Rather, Weber argued that class, status, and power (or party) can be important dimensions behind stratification systems.

neolocal residence   Describes the practice of a newly married couple choosing their place of residence.

nibbana (nirvana)   The supreme goal of Buddhism, in which a person has achieved enlightenment and thereby become liberated from the suffering caused by desire.

nongovernmental organizations (NGOs)   Interest group or welfare type organizations working to solve problems or represent the interests of people not among the most powerful in the society and often neglected by the political system. These organizations, somewhat like nonprofit organizations in the United States, are important in developing nations where the governmental agencies are undeveloped or ineffective.

norms   Basic social rules, usually informal, but essential in guiding social behavior at all levels of the society.

nuclear family   A type of family system most often found in developed societies in which the basic family unit of mother, father, and children are primary and extended relatives from grandparents to aunts, uncles, and so forth have less significance for the family.

parliamentary system   The governmental system currently found in Thailand in which there is a national legislative body composed of representatives. One of the elected representatives from the lower house is selected prime minister, the chief executive of the government. Contrasts with the separation of powers in the United States.

patriarchy   Refers to a society where the father is head of the family and descent and kinship are defined through the male line. Now more generally used to describe any society dominated by men.

patrilineal   A system of tracing descent through the male line and of inheriting property and family identity primarily through one's father.

patrilocal residence Describes the practice of having a newly married couple live with the husband's parents.

political violence Violence systematically used to bring about or prevent social change in a society.

pollution haven A country where, due to lack of regulation, highly polluting industries and toxic waste disposal are concentrated.

polygamy The practice of having more than one spouse at a given time. In the Thai case it refers to the practice of having more than one wife.

popular Buddhism The everyday religion of the vast majority of the Thai people in which traditional beliefs such as animism are thoroughly intermingled with Buddhism.

power In the social stratification theories of Max Weber, power is defined as the ability to achieve goals in the face of opposition from others.

primary groups Small groups with relatively high levels of intimacy and informality. Most sociologists include family groups in the category, as well as groups of friends and other intimate associates. In the simplest hunter/gatherer and horticultural societies, the entire society is a primary group.

revolution The overthrowing of a government by force with the intent of instituting broad social and economic change.

sakdina (dak-di-na) Literally the word(s) meant control over rice fields. During the Ayudhyan period it meant the numeric rank assigned to each individual in society.

samsara The cycle of life death and rebirth in Buddhism, also referred to as *reincarnation*.

Sangha The community of Buddhist monks. In Thailand it also refers to the official organization of the monks under the government.

secondary groups A larger group with a specialized purpose within which people interact on a more impersonal, role-related basis. Most secondary groups, like a sociology class, are limited in time; however, a few, like the Catholic Church, have survived for more than a thousand years.

social stratification The condition in which layered hierarchy and inequality have been hardened or institutionalized, and there is a system of social relationships that determines who gets what and why.

spirit houses Small houses found outside all dwellings in Thailand to show recognition and respect for the spirit of the place to prevent these spirits from reacting angrily to the occupation of their territory.

status Basically this refers to the response given by others to the ranking, high or low, of any individual in a social hierarchy. Social status determines the level of respect and honor individuals commonly are accorded by others.

Sukothai The name of the first old capital of Thailand from A.D. 1253–1350, and consequently the name of this period in Thai history.

Tai   The name of the original people to populate Thailand, believed to have migrated from southern China.

terminal values   Values referring to end states of existence. For any culture, the socially defined goals that individuals in the society should strive to achieve.

Thai   The current name of the dominant ethnic group in Thailand, meaning "free people."

uneven development   Economic development in which some areas of the economy and society develop more rapidly than others, usually the urban areas developing more than rural areas, leading to extensive inequality in the society.

unilineal   A family system in which neither the father's line nor the mother's family line is dominant and defines family relations.

upper class   Old established families with significant ownership of major corporations or land and therefore extensive authority, economic power, and hence status flowing from such ownership, often expressed in tradition of a specific lifestyle.

values   Broad preferences for ideals and beliefs within a society's culture, such as individualism, which shape more specific beliefs, practices, norms, and laws within a society.

wai   The traditional Thai form of greeting with the hands pressed together and raised to show respect while the head is bowed. Reinforces the relative status positions of the individuals, as a subordinate person will raise the hands higher and bow the head more than the superordinate person.

wats   Places of Buddhist worship much like Western churches; found in every community in Thailand.

worldviews   Broad ideologies and perspectives socially developed to explain human behavior and history; found in all societies.

yim   The smile; a means of avoiding conflict in Thai culture is to use a variety of smiles to communicate feelings.

BIBLIOGRAPHY

Akin Rabibhadana. 1993. *Social Inequality: A Source of Conflict in the Future?* Bangkok: Thailand Development Research Institute.

Akin Rabibhadana. 1996. *The Organization of Thai Society in the Early Bangkok Period, 1782–1873*. Bangkok: Amarin Printing.

Akira, Suehiro. 1996. *Capital Accumulation in Thailand, 1855–1985*, Chiang Mai: Silkworm Books.

Akyuz, Yilmaz. 1998. "The East Asian Financial Crisis: Back to the Future." Pp. 33–43 in *Tigers in Trouble*, K. S. Jomo, ed. London: Zed Books.

Anek Laothamatas. 1996. "A Tale of Two Democracies: Conflicting Perceptions of Elections and Democracy in Thailand." Pp. 201–223 in *The Politics of Elections in Southeast Asia*, R. H. Taylor ed. Washington D.C., Woodrow Wilson Center Press and Cambridge University Press.

Apichat Chamratithirong et al. 1995. *National Immigration Survey of Thailand.* Nakhon Pathom, Institute for Population and Social Research, Mahidol University.

Balch, Roger. 1996. "Gridlock Gets Even Worse." *Asian Business Review,* (August 1996, p. 19).

Baltzell, E. Digby. 1958. *Philadelphia Gentlemen: The Making of a National Upper Class*. New York: Free Press.

Bamber, S. D., K. J. Hewison, and P. J. Underwood. 1994. "A History of Sexually Transmitted Diseases in Thailand: Policy and Politics." *Genitourinary Medicine* 69: 148–57.

Bangkok Post. Various issues as cited throughout text.

Barrett, Richard, and Martin King Whyte. 1982. "Dependency Theory and Taiwan: Analysis of a Deviant Case." *American Journal of Sociology* 87: 1064–89.

Bhasshorn Limanonda. 1994. "Family Formation in Rural Thailand: Evidence from the 1989–90 Family and Household Survey." Pp. 383–400 in *Tradition and Change in the Asian Family*, Lee-Jay Cho and Moto Yada, eds. Honolulu: East-West Center.

Bhasshorn Limanonda et al. 1995. *The Summary Report on the General Family Survey*. Bangkok, Institute of Population Studies, Chulalongkorn University.

Bellah, Robert. 1985. *Tokugawa Religion: The Cultural Roots of Modern Japan*. New York: Free Press.

Bellah, Robert N., Richard Madsen, William M. Sullivan, Ann Swidler, and Steven M. Tipton. 1985. *Habits of the Heart: Individualism and Commitment in American Life*. New York: Harper & Row.

Bello, Walden, Shea Cunningham, and Li Kheng Poh. 1998. *A Siamese Tragedy: Development and Disintegration in Modern Thailand*. Bangkok: White Lotus.

Bollen, Kenneth, and Stephen J. Appold. 1993. "National Industrial Structure and the Global System." *American Sociological Review* 58: 283–301.

Bornschier, Volker, and Christopher Chase-Dunn. 1985. *Transnational Corporations and Underdevelopment*. New York: Praeger.

Bornschier, Volker, Christopher Chase-Dunn, and Richard Rubinson. 1978. "Cross-National Evidence of the Effects of Foreign Investment and Aid on Economic Growth and Inequality: A Survey of Findings and a Reanalysis." *American Journal of Sociology* 84: 651–83.

Bornschier, Volker, and Thank-Huyen Ballmer-Cao. 1979. "Income Inequality: A Cross-National Study of the Relationships between MNC-Penetration, Dimensions of the Power Structure and Income Distribution." *American Sociological Review* 44: 487–506.

Brown, Andrew, and Stephen Frenkel. 1993. "Union Unevenness and Insecurity in Thailand." Pp. 82–106 in *Organized Labor in the Asia Pacific Region: A Comparative Study of Trade Unionism in Nine Countries,* Stephen Frenkel, ed. Ithaca, NY: ILR Press.

Callahan, William A. 1998. *Imagining Democracy: Reading "The Events of May" in Thailand.* Singapore: Institute of Asian Studies.

Chai-Anan Samudvanija. 1995. "Economic Development and Democracy." Pp. 235–50 in *Thailand's Industrialization and Its Consequences,* Mehdi Krongkaew, ed. New York: St. Martin's Press.

Chai Podhisata. 1994. "Coresidence and the Transition to Adulthood in the Rural Thai Family." Pp. 363–82 in *Tradition Change in the Asian Family,* Lee-Jay Cho Moto Yada, eds. Honolulu: East-West Center.

Chaiyan Rajchagool. 1994. *The Rise and Fall of the Thai Absolute Monarchy.* Bangkok: White Lotus.

Chase-Dunn, Christopher. 1975. "The Effects of International Economic Dependence on Development and Inequality: A Cross-National Study." *American Sociological Review* 40: 720–38.

Chase-Dunn, Christopher. 1989. *Global Formation: Structures of the World-Economy.* New York: Oxford University Press.

Chirot, Daniel. 1977. *Social Change in the Twentieth Century.* New York: Harcourt Brace Jovanovich.

Chirot, Daniel. 1986. *Social Change in the Modern Era.* New York: Harcourt Brace Jovanovich.

Christensen, Scott R. 1993. *Democracy without Equity?: The Institutions and Consequences of Bangkok-Based Development.* Synthesis Papers vol. III. Bangkok: Thailand Development Research Institute Foundation.

Cohen, Erik. 1991. *Thai Society in Comparative Perspective.* Bangkok: White Lotus.

Dixon, Chris. 1999. *The Thai Economy: Uneven Development and Internationalisation.* London: Routledge.

Domhoff, G. William. 1998. *Who Rules America?: Power and Politics in the Year 2000.* Mountain View, CA: Mayfield.

Dumont, Louis. 1970. *Homo Hierarchieus: The Caste System and Its Implications.* Chicago: University of Chicago Press.

Ehrlich, Richard S. 1994. "Disneyland for Pedophiles." *Freedom Review* 25: 1–2.

Embree, J. F. 1950. "Thailand: A 'Loosely Structured' Social System." *American Anthropologist* 52: 181–93.

Etzioni, Amitai. 1984. *An Immodest Agenda: Rebuilding America before the 21st Century.* New York: McGraw-Hill.

Falkus, Malcolm. 1995. "Thai Industrialization: An Overview." Pp. 13–32 in *Thailand's Industrialization and Its Consequences,* Mehdi Krongkaew, ed. New York: St. Martin's Press.

Fallows, James. 1994. *Looking at the Sun: The Rise of the New East Asian Economic and Political System*. New York: Pantheon.

Gerth, Hans, and C. Wright Mills. 1946. From Max Weber, *Essays in Sociology*. New York: Oxford University Press.

Girling, John L. S. 1981. *Thailand: Society and Politics*. Ithaca, NY: Cornell University Press.

Girling, John L. 1996. *Interpreting Development: Capitalism, Democracy, and the Middle Class in Thailand*. Ithaca, NY: Cornell Southeast Asia Program Publications.

Gohlert, Ernst W. 1991. *Power and Culture: The Struggle Against Poverty in Thailand*. Bangkok: White Lotus.

Gouldner, Alvin, and Richard Peterson. 1962. *Notes on Technology and the Moral Order*. Indianapolis: Bobbs-Merrill.

Guest, Philip. 1994. "Guesstimating the Unestimable: The Number of Child Prostitutes in Thailand." Pp. 72–98 in Orathai Ard-Am and Chanya Sethaput, *Child Prostitution in Thailand: A Documentary Analysis and Estimation of the Number of Child Prostitutes*. Institute for Population and Social Research, Mahidol University.

Hadenius, Axel. 1992. *Democracy and Development*. Cambridge, England: Cambridge University Press.

Hamilton, Gary, and Nicole Biggart. 1988. "Market, Culture, and Authority: A Comparative Analysis of Management and Organization in the Far East." *American Journal of Sociology* 94 (suppl.): S52–S94.

Hata, Tatsuya. 1996. *Bangkok in the Balance*. Bangkok: Duang Prateep Foundation.

Hatch, W., and K. Yamamura. 1996. *Asia in Japan's Embrace: Building a Regional Production Alliance*. Cambridge, England: Cambridge University Press.

Heise, David, Gerhard Lenski, and John Wardwell. 1976. "Further Notes on Technology and the Moral Order." *Social Forces* 55: 316–37.

Hewison, Kenneth. 1993. "Of Regimes, State and Pluralities: Thai Politics Enters the 1990s." Pp. 160–89 in *Southeast Asia in the 1990s: Authoritarianism, Democracy, and Capitalism*, K. Hewison, R. Robison, and G. Rodan, eds. St. Leonards, Australia: Allen and Unwin.

Hill, Hal. 1994. "ASEAN Economic Development: An Analytical Survey—The State of the Field." *Journal of Asian Studies* 53: 832–66.

Hofstede, Geert. 1991. *Cultures and Organization: Software of the Mind*. New York: McGraw-Hill.

Holmes, Henry, and Suchada Tangtongtavy. 1995. *Working with the Thais: A Guide to Managing in Thailand*. Bangkok: White Lotus.

Horowitz, Irving Louis. 1983. *C. Wright Mills: An American Utopian*. New York: Free Press.

Huntington, Samuel. 1996. *The Clash of Civilizations and the Remaking of World Order*. New York: Simon and Schuster.

International Herald Tribune. Various issues as cited throughout text.

Ishii, Yoneo. 1994. "Thai Muslims and the Royal Patronage of Religion." *Law and Society Review* 28: 453–60.

Jackman, Robert. 1975. *Politics and Social Equality: A Comparative Analysis*. New York: John Wiley and Sons.

Johnson, Chalmers. 1982. *MITI and the Japanese Miracle*. Stanford: Stanford University Press.

Jomo, K. S. 1998. "Introduction: Financial Governance, Liberalization and Crises in East Asia." Pp. 1–32 in *Tigers in Trouble*, K. S. Jomo, ed. London: Zed Books.

Kerbo, Harold R. 1996. *Social Stratification and Inequality: Class Conflict in Historical and Comparative Perspective*. 3rd ed. New York: McGraw-Hill.

Kerbo, Harold R., and John McKinstry. 1995. *Who Rules Japan?: The Inner Circles of Economic and Political Power*. Westport, CT: Greenwood/Praeger.

Kerbo, Harold R., and John McKinstry. 1998. *Modern Japan*. New York: McGraw-Hill.

Kerbo, Harold R., and Robert Slagter. 1996. *Japanese and American Corporations in Thailand: Work Organization, Employee Relations, and Cultural Contrasts*. Unpublished manuscript.

Keyes, Charles F. 1989. *Thailand: Buddhist Kingdom as Modern Nation-State*. Boulder, CO: Westview Press.

Khantipalo Bhikko. 1994. *Buddhism Explained: An Introduction to the Teachings of the Lord Buddha*. Chiang Mai, Silkworm Press.

Kim, Eun Nee. 1997. *Big Business, Strong State: Collusion and Conflict in South Korean Development, 1960–1990*. Albany: State University of New York Press.

King, Daniel, and Jim LeGerfo. 1996. "Thailand: Toward Democratic Stability." *Journal of Democracy* 7: 102–17.

Kluckholm, F., and F. L. Strodtbeck. 1960. *Variations in Value Orientations*. Westport, CT: Greenwood Press.

Kuhn, Thomas. 1971. *The Structure of Scientific Revolutions*. 2d ed. Chicago: University of Chicago Press.

Kulick, Elliot, and Dick Wilson. 1996. *Time for Thailand: Profile of a New Success*. Bangkok: White Lotus.

Kunio, Yoshihara. 1994. *The Nation and Economic Growth: The Philippines and Thailand*. Kuala Lumpur: Oxford University Press.

Lenski, Gerhard. 1966. *Power and Privilege*. New York: McGraw-Hill.

Lenski, Gerhard. 1978. "Marxist Experiments in Destratification: An Appraisal." *Social Forces* 57: 364–83.

Lenski, Gerhard, and Patrick Nolan. 1984. "Trajectories of Development: A Test of Ecological-Evolutionary Theory." *Social Forces* 63: 1–23.

Lenski, Gerhard, and Patrick Nolan. 1986. "Trajectories of Development: A Further Test." *Social Forces* 64: 794–95.

Lenski, Gerhard, Jean Lenski, and Partick D. Nolan. 1991. *Human Societies: An Introduction to Macrosociology*. 6th ed. New York: McGraw-Hill.

Levine, Marvin J. 1997. *Worker Rights and Labor Standards in Asia's Four New Tigers: A Comparative Perspective*. New York: Plenum Press

Levine, Robert, Suguru Sato, Tsukasa Hashimoto, and Jyoti Verma. 1995. "Love and Marriage in Eleven Cultures." *Journal of Cross-Cultural Psychology* 26: 554–71.

Lincoln, James R., and Arne L. Kallenberg. 1990. *Culture, Control, and Commitment: A Study of Work Organization and Work Attitudes in the United States and Japan*. New York: Cambridge University Press.

Lipset, Seymour Martin. 1996. *American Exceptionalism: A Double-Edged Sword*. New York: W. W. Norton.

Majapuria, Trilok Chandra. 1993. *Erawan Shrine and Brahma Worship in Thailand*. Bangkok: TecPress Services.

Mastro, Timothy et al. 1994. "Probability of Female to Male Transmission of HIV-1 in Thailand." *The Lancet*: 343, Pp. 204–207.

Mathana Phananirimai and Pawadee Tonguthai. 1994. *Labor Welfare in Thailand.* Bangkok, Thailand Development Research Institute.

Merton, Robert. 1957. *Social Theory and Social Structure.* New York: Free Press.

Muecke, Marjorie A. 1992. "Mother Sold Food, Daughter Sells Her Body: The Cultural Continuity of Prostitution." *Social Science Medicine* 35: 891–901.

Mulder, Neils. 1994. *Inside Thai Society: An Interpretation of Everyday Life.* 4th ed. Bangkok: Editions Duang Kamol.

Mulder, Neils. 1997. *Thai Images: The Culture of the Public World.* Chiang Mai, Thailand: Silkworm Press.

Murray, David. 1996. "The 1995 National Elections in Thailand: A Step Backward for Democracy?" *Asian Survey* 36: 361–75.

Muscat, Robert J. 1994. *The Fifth Tiger: A Study of Thai Development.* Armonk, NY: M. E. Sharpe.

Myrdal, Gunnar. 1970. *The Challenge of World Poverty.* New York: Pantheon.

Napaporn Havanon, Anthony Bennett, and John Knodel. 1993. "Sexual Networking in Provincial Thailand." *Studies in Family Planning* 24, 1–17.

Nation, The. Various issues as cited throughout text.

Nipon Poapongsorn. 1991. "The Informal Sector in Thailand." Pp. 105–44 in *The Silent Revolution: The Informal Sector in Five Asian and Near Eastern Countries,* A. Lawrence Chickering and Mohamed Slahadine eds. San Francisco, ICS Press.

Nolan, Patrick D. 1983. "Status in the World System, Income Inequality, and Economic Growth." *American Journal of Sociology* 89: 410–19.

Nolan, Patrick D. 1983. "Status in the World Economy and National Structure and Development." *International Journal of Contemporary Sociology* 24: 109–20.

Numazaki, Ichiro. 1991. "State and Business in Postwar Taiwan: Comment on Hamilton and Biggart." *American Journal of Sociology* 96: 993–98.

Ockey, James. 1996. "Thai Society and Patterns of Political Leadership." *Asian Survey* 36: 345–60.

Orachai Ard-Am and Chanya Sethaput. B.E. 2537. *Child Prostituion in Thailand: A Documentary Analysis and Estimation of the Number of Child Prostitutes.* Bangkok, Institute for Population and Social Research, Mahidol University.

Osborne, Milton. 1995. *Southeast Asia: An Introductory History.* 6th ed. St. Leonards, Australia: Allen and Unwin.

Panayatou, Theodore, Phanu Kritiporn and Krerkpong Charnpratheep. 1994. "Industrialization and Environment in Thailand: A NIC at What Price." *TDRI Quarterly Review.* 9, 11–17.

Parsons, Talcott. 1953. *The Social System.* New York: Free Press.

Pasuk Phongpaichit. 1982. From *Peasant Girls to Bangkok Masseuses.* Geneva, International Labor Organization.

Pasuk Phongpaichit and Chris Baker. 1996a. *Thailand's Boom.* Chaing Mai, Thailand: Silkworm Books.

Pasuk Phongpaichit and Chris Baker. 1996b. *Thailand: Economy and Politics.* Kuala Lumpur: Oxford University Press.

Pasuk Phongpaichit and Chris Baker. 1998. *Thailand's Boom and Bust.* Chiang Mai, Thailand: Silkworm Books.

Pasuk Phongpaichit and Sungsidh Piryarangsan. 1996. *Corruption and Democracy in Thailand.* Chiang Mai, Silkworm Books.

Pfeiffer, John. 1977. *The Emergence of Society: A Prehistory of the Establishment.* New York: McGraw-Hill.

Phillips, Herbert P. 1966. *Thai Peasant Personality: The Patterning of Interpersonal Behavior in the Village of Bang Chan.* Berkeley: University of California Press.

Portes, Alejandro. 1976. "On the Sociology of National Development: Theories and Issues." *American Journal of Sociology* 85: 55–85.

Pranee Tinakorn. 1995. "Industrialization and Welfare: How Poverty and Income Distribution Are Affected." Pp. 218–31 in *Thailand's Industrialization and Its Consequences,* Mehdi Krongkaew, ed. New York: St. Martin's Press.

Prudhisan Jumbala. 1992. *Nation Building and Democratization in Thailand: A Political History.* Bangkok: Chulalongkorn University Social Research Institute.

Pye, Lucien W. 1985. *Asian Power and Politics: The Cultural Dimensions of Authority.* Cambridge, MA: Harvard University Press.

Ragin, Charles, and David Zaret. 1983. "Theory and Method in Comparative Strategies." *Social Forces.* 61: 731–54.

Redman, Charles. 1978. *The Rise of Civilization.* San Francisco: Freeman.

Reynolds, Craig J. 1987. *Thai Radical Discourse. The Real Face of Thai Feudalism Today.* Ithaca, NY: Cornell Southeast Asia Program.

Riggs, Fred W. 1966. *Thailand: The Modernization of a Bureaucratic Polity.* Honolulu: East-West Center Press.

Ritzer, George. 1996. *Sociological Theory.* New York: McGraw-Hill.

Robertson, Philip S., Jr. 1996. "The Rise of the Rural Network Politician: Will Thailand's New Elite Endure?" *Asian Survey* 36, no. 9 (September 1996): 924–41.

Rohlen, Thomas P. 1982. *Japan's High Schools.* Berkeley: University of California Press.

Rokeach, M. 1979. "Change and Stability on American Value Systems, 1968–71" in *Understanding Human Values: Individual and Societal,* M. Rokeach ed. New York, The Free Press.

Rostow, Walter. 1960. *The Stages of Economic Growth.* New York: Cambridge University Press.

Sachs, Jeffrey. 1997. "The Wrong Medicine for Asia." *New York Times,* November 3.

Sachs, Jeffrey. 1998. "The IMF and the Asian Flu." *The American Prospect* 17, March–April.

Sadoff, Claudia W. 1994. "The Value of Thailand's Forests." *TDRI Quarterly Review* 9, 18–23.

Sanitsuda Ekachai. 1994. *Seeds of Hope: Local Initiatives in Thailand.* Bangkok: Thai Development Support Committee.

Schell, Orville. 1994. *Mandate of Heaven.* New York: Simon and Schuster.

Seagrave, Sterling. 1995. *Lord's of the Rim.* London: Transworld Publishers, Corgi Books.

Sesser, Stan. 1993. "The Course of Corruption: The Place of Golf in Thai Society." *Mother Jones* 18: 44–55.

Shapiro, Andrew L. 1992. *We're Number One: Where America Stands—and Falls—in the New World Order.* New York: Vintage Books.

Shearer, Alistair. 1989. *Thailand: The Lotus Kingdom.* London: John Murray.

Skrobanek, S. 1987. "Strategies against Prostitution in Thailand." In *Third World: Second Sex,* M. Davies ed. New Jersey, Zed Books.

Smelser, Neil J. 1976. *Comparative Methods in the Social Sciences.* Englewood Cliffs, N.J.: Prentice-Hall.

Snyder, David, and Edward Kick. 1979. "Structural Position in the World System and Economic Growth, 1955–1970: A Multiple Analysis of Transnational Interactions." *American Journal of Sociology* 84: 1096–128.

Somboon Suksamran. 1993. *Buddhism and Political Legitimacy.* Bangkok: Chulalongkorn University Research Report Series No. 2.

Sompop Manarungsan. 1989. *Economic Development in Thailand, 1850–1950.* Bangkok, Chulalongkorn University.

Somrudee Nicro. 1993. "Thailand's NIC Democracy: Studying From General Elections. *Pacific Affairs* 66, 167–82.

Somsak Tambunlernchai. 1993. "Manufacturing." Pp. 118–50 in *The Thai Economy in Transition,* Peter G. Warr ed. Cambridge, Cambridge University Press.

Stokes, Randall, and David Jaffee. 1982. "Another Look at the Export of Raw Materials and Economic Growth." *American Sociological Review* 47: 402–7.

Suntaree Komin. 1989. *Social Dimensions of Industrialization in Thailand.* Bangkok, National Institute of Development Administration.

Suntaree Komin. 1991. *Psychology of the Thai People: Values and Behavior Patterns.* Bangkok, National Institute of Development Administration.

Suntaree Komin. 1995. "Changes in Social Values in the Thai Society and Economy: A Post-Industrialization Scenario." Pp. 251–66 in *Thailand's Industrialization and its Consequences,* Mehdi Krongkaew ed. New York, St. Martin's Press, Inc.

Terwiel, B. J. 1991. *A Window on Thai History.* Bangkok: Editions Duang Kamol.

Thurow, Lester. 1991. *Head to Head: The Coming Economic Battle between the United States, Japan, and Europe.* New York: Morrow.

Unger, Danny. 1998. *Building Social Capital in Thailand: Fibers, Finance, and Infrastructure.* Cambridge: Cambridge University Press.

Vogel, Ezra. 1989. *One Step Ahead in China: Guangdong under Reform.* Cambridge, MA: Harvard University Press.

Vogel, Ezra. 1991. *The Four Little Dragons: The Spread of Industrialization in East Asia.* Cambridge, MA: Harvard University Press.

Wallerstein, Immanual. 1974. *The Modern World System: Capitalist Agriculture and the Origins of the European World-Economy in the 16th Century.* New York: Academic Press.

Wallerstein, Immanual. 1980. *The Modern World System II: Mercantilism and the Consolidation of the European World-Economy, 1600–1750.* New York: Academic Press.

Wallerstein, Immanual. 1989. *The Modern World System III: The Second Era of Great Expansion of the Capitalist World-Economy, 1730–1840s.* New York: Academic Press.

Walpola Sri Rahula. 1988. *What the Buddha Taught.* Bangkok, Haw Trai Foundation.

Walters, Pamela Barnhouse, and Richard Rubinson. 1983. "Educational Expansion and Economic Output in the United States, 1890–1996: A Production Function Analysis." *American Sociological Review* 48: 480–93.

Warr, Peter G. Ed. 1993. *The Thai Economy in Transition.* Cambridge: Cambridge University Press.

Warr, Peter G. and Bhanupong Nidhiprabha. 1996. *Thailand's Economic Miracle: Stable Adjustment and Sustained Growth.* Kuala Lumpur, Oxford University Press.

Wathinee Boonchalaski and Philip Guest. 1994. *Prostitution in Thailand.* Nakhon Pathom, Institute for Population and Social Research, Mahidol University.

World Bank. 1996. *World Development Report 1996: From Plan to Market.* New York: Oxford University Press.

World Bank. 1999. *World Development Report, 1998–1999.* New York: Oxford University Press.

Wu, Y. and C. Wu. 1980. *Economic Development in Southeast Asia: The Chinese Dimension.* Stanford, CA, Standford University Press.

Wyatt, David K. 1984. *Thailand: A Short History.* New Haven: Yale University Press.

Preface

http://coombs.anu.edu.au/WWWVL-AsianStudies.html   A site produced by the Research School of Pacific and Asian Studies, the Australian National University, Canberra, Australia, in conjunction with 38 other organizations, this is the ultimate guide to academic resources in Asian studies. Of special note is the listing of e-journals with contents published online.

Chapter 1

Newspapers

http://www.bangkokpost.com and *http://www.nationmultimedia.com* Web sites of the *Bangkok Post* and *The Nation*, both English language newspapers published daily in Bangkok. Many excellent articles on current events, social problems, and business and economics. Daily reading begins to give some flavor of life in the country from an urban middle-class perspective. A useful exercise is to read some articles of interest and think about what is surprising about what has been read.

Asian Institute of Technology

http://www.ait.ac.th/Asia/asia.html   A gateway to many Asian Web sites. Has a clickable map; click on Thailand and find your way to many worthwhile sites.

King Mongkut Institute of Technology

http://pundit.ce.kmitl.ac.th   Another good gateway to many Thai sites.

Chapter 2

http://www.mahidol.ac.th/Thailand/Thailand-main.html   The official Web site of Thailand, lots of useful information but all provided by government agencies or government corporations. This is an example: "On 23 February 1991, the National Peace Keeping Council (NPKC), led by General Sundhorn Kongsompong, the Supreme Commander of the Royal Thai Armed Forces, took over the administration of the country with the objective of strengthening democratic processes through a revised constitution. The takeover of administration was peaceful and widely endorsed by the people and the media." Read between the lines, always.

Chapter 3

Business Day

http://bday.net   A business daily published by a Singapore firm that contains lots of current economic and business news.

Bank of Thailand

http://www.bot.or.th   The Web site of the Bank of Thailand has extensive economic data updated monthly and some descriptions of current policy. Be sure to click on the English button on the upper right of the home page.

Stock Exchange of Thailand (SET)

http://www.set.or.th   A window on the volatile Thai stock market. You can check market moves overall and in various sectors of the economy. Downloadable data and many links to other financial and economic sites on the internet.

Chapter 4

Thailand the Big Picture

http://www. nectec.or.th   The National Electronics and Computer Technology Center (NECTEC) is a research organization operated under the National Science and Technology Development Agency. This server maintains a list of Internet servers (domestic and abroad) that contains information pertaining to Thailand. From this site you can select a directory of all government agency home pages, including the two listed below, and many other interesting sites.

The Thai Government Home Page

http://www.thaigov.go.th   Useful descriptions of government structure and some policies.

Parliament

http://www.parliament.go.th   The Thai parliament, including a directory of political parties and number of members in parliament.

Chapter 5

The World Bank

http://www.worldbank.org   Not the easiest site to navigate, but many extracts from the *World Development Report* are available here.

Chapter 6

http://www.ciolek.com/WWWVL-Buddhism.html   Part of the WWW virtual
library; links to many Buddhist Studies sites.

Chapter 8

Coalition Against Prostitution, Child Abuse and Trafficking

http://www.capcat.ksc.net   This organization provides quite a bit of information and links to organizations based and working in Thailand as well
as to international organizations combating prostitution and especially
child prostitution.

Thailand Environment Institute

http://www.tei.or.th

Pollution Control Department

http://www.pcd.go.th   Daily updates on air quality in Bangkok as well as
data from other regions of the country.

United Nations Development Program

http://www.undp.org/popin/regional/asiapac/asiapac.htm   Lots of data on
population and trends in Asia, including Thailand.

United Nations AIDS Organization

http://www.unaids.org   This site has lots of good data and discussion on
the world wide AIDS epidemic as well as information on specific countries and prevention strategies that have worked. When you go to this
site wait a few seconds and it will transfer you to the active Web page.

NAME INDEX

SUBJECT INDEX

AIDS, 108, 112–114
American corporations in Thailand, 73
animism, 13, 16, 80–81, 85
anthropocentric, 82
Asian development model, 42–43
Asian economic crisis, 31–32, 46–48
Asian value systems, 9–11
Ayudhya, 14
    history of, 18–21

Bangkok period,
    early history of, 22–25
    recent history, 25–27
Bhumibol Adulyadej, King (Rama IX),
    52, 70
Buddhism, 2, 6, 13, 79, 81–89
    in everyday life, 84–88
    organization of, 88–89
    popular, 87
bunkhun, 8–9

capitalist development
    state, 41
caste system, 64
Chakri dynasty, 21
China, Tiananmen Square massacre, 49
Chinese
    in Thai economy, 44, 71
    in Thailand, 75
Chulalongkorn, King (Rama V), 22, 24,
    103, 115, 116
class, 63
Cold War, 27–28
collectivist value system, 10
corporate class, 69–72
corruption as social problem, 114–115
corvee system, 20
coup, 25
CP Group, 71
culture, definition, 5
culture shock, 63

demographic transition, 107

economic development
    in Asia, 40–43
    in Thailand, 38–40, 43–46
education
    for economic development, 102–103
    quality of, 100–101
    in Thailand, 99–104
elections, in Thailand, 53–54
End Child Prostitution
    in Asian Tourism (ECPAT), 108
estate system, 17
ethnic groups, definition, 2
European powers, and Thailand, 23–25
export-oriented industrialization, 43

face, 4
family
    definition of, 92
    extended, 92
    as master institution, 91
    nuclear, 92
    in Thailand, 76, 90–95
feudalism, 17
Forum For the Poor, 69
Free Thai Movement, 26–27
functional alternatives, 72
functional imperatives, 32

gender
    relations, 73
    socialization, 94–95
genocide, 75
Grand Palace, 14, 73
green revolution, 68
gross domestic product (GDP), 34, 36–37

hill tribes, 2, 75–76, 121n

ideal types, 64
import substitution industrialization, 43
income inequality
    comparative, 67